HAVE I
TAUGHT YOU
EVERYTHING
I KNOW?

HAVE I
TAUGHT YOU
EVERYTHING
I KNOW?

Diane Fay Skomars

Blessings,
Di Fay Skomars

MILL CITY PRESS

Copyright © 2014 by Diane Fay Skomars

Mill City Press, Inc.
322 First Avenue N, 5th floor
Minneapolis, MN 55401
612.455.2293
www.millcitypublishing.com

ISBN-13: 978-1-62652-691-4
LCCN: 2014902140

Book Design by Kristeen Ott

Printed in the United States of America

Dedicated to Monette Fay Magrath
and to those who suffered on 9/11.

FOREWORD

Everyone has a story to tell if they were in New York City on September 11, 2001. Everyone still remembers the moment they heard the news about the first plane slamming into the World Trade Center Building. Everyone who survived the inferno was deeply affected and profoundly changed. Here's my story as I lived it that Tuesday in Manhattan.

Business Network International (BNI) met every Tuesday at 7 a.m. near Lexington Avenue. Promoting each other's business (insurance agent, financial advisor, telephone company rep., dentist, lawyer, doctor, banker, photographer, personal trainer, podiatrist, and others) was our goal. We were an active chapter and our meetings were lively. So it was on September 11th. Walking back from the meeting to my studio of photography on 7th Avenue, I remember the beauty of the morning. The air was crisp and the sky was bluer than blue. My mom (Nana) would have called it a "bonnie day."

The first time I heard the news was from a client who visited my studio to plan a photographic shoot. He wanted to know if I had heard about the small plane that nicked the World Trade Center. Neither of us knew much more but when he left, I turned on my radio. I had no television in my studio. Throughout that morning the news was very confusing on Manhattan's radio stations. Public radio was out and the only station I could get was "talk radio" warning of a cloud over the city that could be toxic.

It was my daughter, Monette, who called me from Los Angeles and stopped my heart with the news about the Twin Towers. She was the one who asked me, "What flight is Max on from Newark?" My husband was to take off at 8:28 a.m. on a United flight heading West.

The next couple of hours are a blur but certain memories are crystal clear. It was such a comfort to hear from my brother, Buzz, who urged me to "fill the studio's bathtub with water, buy as much food as possible from the deli downstairs, and place a towel on the floor at the base of the door." I remember praying on my knees on a Persian rug I bought at a Chelsea flea market with my friend Rose. My cell phone was out, but my ground line was working, and I waited for Max to call. As we were talking, my daughter and I were sobbing, believing it could be our last conversation.

At that moment of clarity when the future looked so bleak and I felt I was faced with my own mortality and Max's and the possible mortality of the greatest city on earth, I asked Monette, **"Have I taught you everything I know?"**

Fortunately, it was not the end of the city, or Max, or me, but it was a life defining moment. Max called about noon; although his plane had been on the tarmac third in line to take off, Newark Airport had been shut down and he was home safe. Later, when I felt it was okay to leave the phone, I walked down Seventh Avenue until I saw a couple of people with the "dust of death" on them. I have been asked many times, "Why didn't you take photographs?" Couldn't do it. A portrait photographer does not a photojournalist make.

During the following year, the phrase, "Have I taught you everything I know?" haunted me. Had I? In 2003 I decided to write a page a day and give it to Monette for Christmas. I wanted to make sure that if something happened to me, I would have passed on what I wanted her to know. She told me she couldn't read it for a long time but when she finally did, she laughed and cried throughout. The next Christmas, Monette gave the journal back to me and said, "Publish it when you retire."

The tenth anniversary year of the events of 9/11 has come and gone. If I, who suffered no personal harm, lost no one to death, and was able to return home late that same day can still recall how I felt in my tiny studio receiving bits and pieces of truth...I can only imagine how the others felt who really suffered and still do. We must never forget. And we must continue to teach what we know. Here, then, is a year of lessons, reminders, and wishes for my daughter.

January 1, 2003

"White Rabbit!" You got me!

****

"Rabbit Rabbit Rabbit" 1987 Cynthia Thomas

> "When 'rabbit, rabbit, rabbit'
> are the first words you say
> at the start of each month
> on the very first day,
> then throughout the year,
> if you make this a habit,
> you'll be covered for sure
> with the luck of the rabbit."

For over twenty years on the first day of every month, you and I have been calling each other with "White Rabbit" to receive good luck from the other. It is a tradition borrowed from our friend Bob in Missouri and fun to keep alive. (Note: Bob's version is "White Rabbit.") Since you dwell on the West Coast and I am planted in the Mid-West, we have rules that govern this ritual. We must do it in "real time" and not stoop to leaving a message. The problem is that you can see my incoming call and can usually beat me to the punch. (Max will have already gotten me at 12:01 a.m.) How quickly the month goes by and soon we are back again to "White Rabbiting."

Today is special for another reason because it is the start of this project to write a message-a-day to you for a year. It seems a rather daunting assignment, but I am determined to write down what I know for you. Before 9/11, I believed a momma taught all lessons by example; no need to talk about it. But now I realize it is okay to leave some advice, observations and lessons behind in writing. Except for work-related memos, I am not a writer, so this self-imposed assignment is a struggle for me, big time!

As you read, please take along a sieve to gather a few grains of truth you may wish to remember, knowing the rest will fall away.

January 2, 2003

"Illumination"

It's late evening - a long day at work. My thoughts run along these lines:

> "If everyone lit just one little candle,
> what a bright world this would be."

(From the song "One Little Candle,"
music by George Mysels and lyrics by Joseph Maloy Roach)

It would be grand if each person was able and willing to "shine a light" to help us see, really see, the universe, behind dark corners, and into the faces of others. Candles seem to give off the best light, create the softest illumination, and manifest a welcoming atmosphere. Think back to your birthdays with candles on the cake; Christmas Eve in a church aglow with candlepower; the candles you light while tub bathing; the tapers lit for a dinner party. Candles don't just pierce the darkness, they draw us to the light; they make us slow down, take stock, feel better.

Go light a candle right now and realize its power, its warmth, its attraction. Absorb the light and pass it on. Are you glowing?

Do you make the world a brighter place with your own light, Monette? How do you do so?

"Never Go To Sleep in Anger."

If I want to stay awake half the night, all I have to do is try to fall asleep in anger. Tonight is such a night.

I came home to find all my important personal things (albums, cameras, writings, gifts and wrap, tchotchkes, framed photographs, books, personal computer, candles to calm, teddy bears from you and Nana) in the middle of the living room. Max had moved them to make room for his stuff in the study. "If I am home most days, I need to create my own space." It sounded rational but felt bad. My most important things in a heap in the living room! I was hurt and angry. Our living quarters are so small and I felt insignificant. He hadn't even discussed it before acting.

Alas, I worked hard at finding appropriate anger words but mostly I blew it. I finally calmed down and said how it made me feel. We made up, and we both finally slept.

How do you handle your anger? Does anything good ever come from it?

"A Stage Dress Awaits Your Return"

Today I worked in our cottage from morning 'til dusk. Max continues to rearrange the back room so he can "work more efficiently." This generally means turning doors into desks and adding shelves everywhere! The man is on a mission.

Instead of putting away my treasures left in the living room, I spent hours going over photographs from your childhood. Could remember every occasion, what you did and said, how you smelled (every mother knows her child's fragrance) and conjectured about what you were thinking. Since you were highly verbal, I usually knew what you thought. It was delicious to review your life. It invoked such a strong, yet soft, response in me.

Later I found a stage dress from some play you were in. I hand-washed it and ironed it and let it hang as if awaiting your return. Am almost grateful my stuff got piled in the living room because I got to touch each item and remember.

Sometimes you have to shake up your "stuff" to remember where you have been, and to connect with what is important.

Remember to "shake up your stuff" from time to time and see where it takes you, My Dear.

"Chicken Soup"

This is a chicken soup story, sort of.

After fussing about not wanting to attend a party (i.e. it's a weekend and the event felt like work; I'm an introvert and hate large groups; I don't want to dress up), I decided we had better attend. I'd wear your scarf for "protection."

Alas, I called the host's home to say we were coming and found out her husband had just been hospitalized and the party was called off! She seemed so stressed, I offered to call the guests. I had to scramble to locate telephone numbers but got the job done.

Later we drove to Duluth and brought the family chicken soup from the night before. He's now home from the hospital, thank goodness.

Moral: Say "yes" to the invitation because it may be called off and the only price is chicken soup.

DIANE FAY SKOMARS

"Finns are Known for Their HARD Work."

Today is a Monday and I look forward to work. At age 11, my first job was as a babysitter to the Lee family with five great kids. I then hooked up with my girlfriend Molly and we made hot pads at 10 cents a piece and sold them door to door until one of us accidentally sewed our finger on the sewing machine and our business was shut down. Later, my friend Gail and I went house to house with Christmas cards from the Cheerful Card Company and made enough to cover our holiday gift buying. During high school and college I sold children's clothing and jewelry at Wahl's Department Store, and bridal dresses at Maurice's. After the university, I taught third grade at a Roman Catholic grade school and loved going to mass with the class to start each day.

Next I began my long career in higher education and, except for those years in New York as a photographer, I have devoted most of my professional life to universities. I found my niche. How did you find your niche?

In our family the highest compliment one can receive is, "She is a hard worker." You have inherited the work ethic. When I think of all you have accomplished while keeping your dream alive, I stand in awe.

"Therapy"

"You have the tendency, based on the past, to suppress your own thoughts to stay in accord with others."

This morning I had a long distance telephone session with my NY therapist. It was marvelous to hear her voice, her laugh and her counsel. At one point, I asked her what I had - what I suffered from - what was my "disease?" She responded with the above. I can truly say this woman gave me hope and a new life when I felt so lonely and disconnected in New York City. Every Wednesday night my therapy group met to discuss how we felt about each other - and they weren't buying Minnesota nice! This was very hard work, but I grew in new ways and, in time, found my voice.

I like the concise nature of her statement. It doesn't seem as scary as it feels at times. It explains a lot. As strong-minded as I am, I will often resort to this safe harbor - to my own detriment.

What is your m.o., Monette? How does it look to you? How does it feel?

"Bilin and Rose"

One of the smartest and kindest women I know is a Chinese Japanese American. Bilin was born in Seattle and works as a lead administrator in higher education in Minnesota. Tonight she told us in book club that people often ask her where she is from. When she responds, "Seattle," they ask her, "No, where are you *really* from?" And it is not always friendly.

This came up at my book club tonight because we had read *To Kill a Mocking Bird* and had a discussion about race. As our friend Rose Nolen (author and award-winning columnist) taught you and me years ago when we brought her with us from Missouri for a visit to God's Country, "Northern Minnesota is no paradise; everyone stares at me because I am African American." Rose taught me about race, but she also taught me about how to live a purposeful life. (Look up Rose Nolen on the Internet to read more about her accomplishments.) I am blessed to count her as my friend.

I also recall from that trip that it was September and our motel was celebrating "October Fest" early, in case of bad weather later. We awoke hearing a small band playing German "oompa" music and smelling bratwursts on the grill. And it was snowing buckets! Rose said she probably will not be back to Northern Minnesota any time soon.

What do you recall about the trip from Columbia to Duluth?

"Wally Funk"

A Stephens College graduate, Wally Funk is one of the most remarkable people I know. (We met when I was the Alumni Director at Stephens.) In 1961, at the age of 21, she volunteered for the "Women in Space" program and after vigorous tests, she became the youngest member of the "Mercury Thirteen." These thirteen women made personal and professional sacrifices to participate and successfully complete 87 different tests in phase one of three phases (the same ones for men and women) including swallowing a three foot rubber hose for a stomach test and floating for hours in an isolation tank of warm water that removed the senses and simulated weightlessness. Wally floated for a record 10 hours and 35 minutes. All this was done in secret because we seemed to be in a race with the Russians. In 1963 the Soviets sent Cosmonaut Valentina Tereshkova into space and our female astronaut program was suspended for twenty years.

Wally went on to a distinguished career in aviation and stands fit and ready to go into space. Living our dream is what we have in this life, Monette. When you get discouraged look up www.wallyfly.com and read about a woman who never, ever gives up.

DIANE FAY SKOMARS

January 10, 2003

"The Nature of Nature"

Winter has its wondrous side with crystal clear nights, brazenly blue skies and air so fresh it stops your heart when you breathe in deeply. Winter, the most feared of all the seasons in the North, surprises us often with plenty of bright sunshine pouring through our windows and helping us forget the 20 degrees below zero outside.

While others in the country discuss the President, Trent Lott, and Iraq, we talk about the weather. "Cold" is rarely used in conversation. Only "brisk," "chilly," and "there's a nip in the air."

When my mom, Nana to you, moved to San Diego, she never stopped reporting on the weather every day, even though the temperature fluctuated about four degrees. Born and raised in Northern Minnesota, Nana told me to wear a scarf when I walked in her California neighborhood in 75 degrees. I believe she thought the wind might change and we would experience a "Northeaster off Lake Superior," even in San Diego!

How does weather affect you? Do you have enough variety in Pasadena to experience four seasons?

In the words of Nana, "Always button up!"

"UMD Women's Ice Hockey"

After dining with friends, we attended a women's hockey game: UMD vs. Dartmouth. It was a religious experience for me!

These women are strong skaters and when they take command, they pass that puck between them as if it was attached by string to their sticks going smoothly back-and-forth down the rink. I was raised to look for the "break away," the super star who stole the puck and the show. At tonight's game, I began to realize that the team approach was much more interesting to watch. And because it didn't call on just one or two to shine, it taught real teamwork - - often touted in the male world as the only way to understand life.

Tonight these women, my UMD team, skated like the strong, smooth athletes they are. It matters not the gender; it matters only the skill. Will we ever learn?

Do you remember how to skate? What have you learned from being on a team?

"I Am My Own Best Company."

Do you ever grant a day to yourself? This was one of those delicious days - all to myself.

Up at 7 a.m. Toothpaste and back exercise. Hot tea and dry cereal. Long walk in the cold - two hats, mittens and gloves, scarf and heavy boots. (6 below plus a strong wind.) To town for the newspapers and breakfast at the Vanilla Bean Cafe with friends Jan and Paul.

Snowshoeing and home to go over holiday cards and correct addresses while watching videos: *To Kill a Mocking Bird* and *The King and I*.

Exercise tape, split pea soup for supper and talks with the Max by phone. He is on the road with his ragtime show. Miss that guy!

Feed the cat and crash but not before leaving a message for my girl. I love you.

Are you your own best company?

January 13, 2003

"If the Daughter's Happy, the Mother's Happy."

We spoke tonight and you sounded so happy. You are busy packing and planning for your Washington D.C. play, *Book of Days* at Arena Stage.

I love the sound of your voice. Nana used to say she could always tell if I was sad, mad, glad, tired, happy, distracted, rested, down or up just by the *tone* of my voice. I now understand it and can tell everything I need to know by the sound of yours.

When I visit a store and hear a girl call out, "Mom," I still turn around thinking it is my Monette.

You and I made a plan to meet in NYC in March. We can catch a show, get our nails done, shop, hit the Met, eat popcorn for lunch at a movie. Who could ask for anything more?

Lucky me to claim you as daughter.

DIANE FAY SKOMARS

January 14, 2003

"A Long Day's Journey Into Night" (title borrowed from Eugene O'Neil)

Up at 4 a.m. and on the road at 4:45. It is always a long day to the Twin Cities and back when done in one day. Love the morning - even in the dark. Will return at night in the dark.

You, my dear, don't like mornings! I remember hating to wake you in the morning light. Stroking your sweet nose, listening to your plea to, "Wake me in 10 minutes and I promise I'll get up." My threat would be to send Bandit in to lick your face with his foul, doggy breath.

Those were sweet times in Columbia, MO. We had a peaceful house and there was a good ebb and flow to our days. Me, up early to fix your breakfast and pack your lunch, feed the cat, take a run with Bandit on a leash, and then to wake you. You, up and grabbing breakfast, looking great, gathering papers and books for class, and we'd roar out to get you to school on time until you drove yourself. After school, I'd get you to the horse barn where you would groom and ride your beloved horse, Trustee, with exceptional coach Sarah near by.

What do you remember, you, who fill a room with your presence?

"Blah, Blah, Blah"

The cold winter continues well below zero. Hard to believe it can be so numbing by the lake in the wind. Easy to get the "blahs" especially when I stay inside.

The only way to fight the blahs is to start my engine and get moving; exercise. So, when I finish this writing, I will go through my exercises: 20 round trips on the stairs, 10 rounds of weight lifts, exercise tape for 40 minutes. I will feel good or at least better.

I look out and I see two deer. A mom and her yearling. The doe keeps a keen eye out for her own and together they prance back into the woods. Sort of like you and me. Our life imitates nature.

Did you "move" today? Did you meet nature face to face? What did you learn?

"Working with Millionaires"

I wrote a proposal today for millions of dollars. I don't know if this project will get funded, but it was exciting to add all those zeros.

I used to be afraid of folks with big money but I learned they were as smart and dull, bold and scared, sane and crazy as the rest of us.

Some of the loveliest people I've ever met have oodles of money and lots of class. Have also spent time with poor folks where the same thing applies. Many are lovely and classy.

So, money doesn't decide our fate unless we are without food, shelter, and a job.

Despite the zeros in your bank account, do you feel rich or poor, you actress, you?

"On Driving Through a Blizzard."

    Tonight I drove through a blizzard to get to St. Paul, and I will fly to NY tomorrow. A good snow blizzard brings out the best in me. There are, however, certain rules associated with driving on ice when you can't see for the flakes:

1. Always have a full tank of gas!
2. Warm up your car 5-10 minutes before the trip (the car experts say "no" and I say, "Are you crazy?")
3. Travel with extra hats, mittens, jacket, blanket, scarf, flare, flashlight, food, water. Also, look good--in case they find you frozen solid!
4. Put a bright ball at the top of your extended antenna so they can locate you if a drift covers your stalled car.
5. Do not keep the car running if stalled. Turn it off and keep moving inside the car. Add layers. Pray.
6. A cell phone helps.
7. Don't get out of the car for any reason.
8. If you are still driving, follow a truck. They keep moving no matter what.
9. Drive in second if the going is slow.
10. Call your mom.

DIANE FAY SKOMARS

"I Travel for Its Own Sake."

A person is either a traveler or not. I live to go somewhere. Anywhere.

I love the preparation, the maps, the planning, the uncertainty, the adventure. I love the road, the water, the sky, the tracks. I guess I love the movement. I have been to over 60 countries, many more than once, and I am still counting.

How do you feel about travel, you who were on 23 airplanes by age three; you who were made an honorary Laplander at the Arctic Circle above Finland; you who have travelled by horseback and waterway, railroad tracks and parasailing; you who crossed the country in our old Toyota?

Where do you want to go next? What is stopping you?

"A Close Friend is a Gift."

All my life, there was a close friend just around the corner. I have been that fortunate. And then I moved to NY and learned a close friend is a gift, not a given.

You will remember that my friend Donna and I shared a trip to Viet Nam with four other women. Today she and I saw the film, *The Quiet American* that takes place in Viet Nam. Because of the experience we shared traveling, we have formed a lovely friendship based on mutual interests in Buddhism, travel and politics.

I used to think I had to have a best friend. But I gave that up. Now I draw strength, insight, and support from a variety of people.

How do you find a friend and keep one? And when did you learn to let one go?

"One Can Only be in One Place at a Time."

How can I love our Lake Superior cottage with the same intensity as our NY, one bedroom apartment? Because both are exceptional dwellings. Each feeds my soul. And they are in stark contrast to each other. From solitude to frenzy, from nature's best to the nature of people. What does our chosen space and place say about each of us? And do we really choose our abode, or does life and circumstance nudge us to find the right place to alight?

Are you in California by choice? If you could live anywhere, where would it be? If opportunity and finances were positive, what place would you select to create a new life? I hope you will feel free to try some place new.

"Below Zero"

It is 15 below zero today on the shore of Lake Superior. The little propane heater pumps its heart out, keeping hot air circulating. The cat's hair stands at attention with an electrical charge. The term "Frozen North" is no lie.

The car is plugged into an electrical outlet, but still the engine whines before turning over and finally moving like a frozen robot. Because of the cold, the tires have a flat side, so the ride is bumpity-bump. Max proves his love each day when he starts my car, makes me cappuccino, and then moons me as the snow swirls around his bare ass. I laugh all the way to work in Duluth!

It is so crazy to live here. Four seasons indeed, all extreme. Never forget, you, too, were born in the North on the shore of the mighty Mississippi River, in Minneapolis. You experienced the bitter cold of winter for the first ten years of your life.

What do you say when someone asks you where you are from?

"Heather Cooke"

Write down the name of your first pet. _____

Then write down the name of the first street where you lived. _____

Put those two names together and it is the name of your "lounge act" character.

_____

Isn't that funny? Max's answer is "Fifi Cascade." Perfect. Mine is "Heather Cooke." Feeling silly today despite the extreme cold and a long day at work.

Do you feel silly often enough to counter the heavy days?

"Olive You"

Today I will tell you what I love about you.

I love it that you called me today on your cell phone and told me the highs and lows of the first rehearsal days in D.C.

I love it that you care about what you do and it's not just about "another job."

I love it that you could tell your L.A. friend to consider keeping a baby even though the baby stands a good chance of being a Downs Syndrome child. You told me you imagined their little one could teach them how to receive and give love in incredible ways.

I love your clarity of thought and your compassion for the lost and the lonely, and your dedication to your art.

I love you! Or as you learned in your role in the film, *The Other Sister*, "Olive You!"

"Never Send Your Mate Alone to the Grocery Store"

He will get chicken breasts instead of chicken thighs.

He will pick up iceberg lettuce even if you write down romaine.

He will buy green peppers no matter what you told him about the new recipe requiring yellow and red.

He will bring home ice cream with 18% butterfat in spite of the fact you are in Weight Watchers.

He will forget the Kleenex holders are all square and he will arrive home with rectangular boxed tissues, lots of them.

He will announce olives with pits were on sale and forget you needed stuffed green olives for the hot dish.

He will always buy the cheapest cat food ignoring the fact that your feline eats only chicken in gravy and hates fish of any kind.

He will never, ever bring home your favorite shampoo, personal feminine products, or curlers. Don't even list these items. Too risky.

God bless him for trying, but never send your mate to the grocery store.

"God is Good"

These two words, "God" and "good," are so close to each other and seem right. I never mind assigning good to God. All that is good does feel like God.

It's so personal but I do believe in God.

When ALL else fails...

When I am down and out...

When I want to eat worms and die...

I say, "I can't take another step...."

"Can't take more bad news..."

"Can't breathe..."

and finally, "Can't go it alone."

I abandon self and get down on my bad knees and ask for help from God by saying, "Please, please help me, God." And a small peace comes over me and eventually I get back to living. How is it for you?

"Snow Day"

Today was a day off. Slow to rise, cappuccino in bed, newspapers to read, cat Esme to stroke.

No walk outside because it is way below zero with a wind off Lake Superior. But we don't care. The Max made breakfast and it was a feast:

Corn Pancakes (from corn muffin mix)

Heated Syrup (local)

Fruit Compote (no cans used)

Crisp Bacon

Yum!

Then hot baths and oil back rubs.

A long afternoon nap while a large turkey roasted filling the cottage with promise.

Watched a classic movie. The day seemed to go on and on and on.

I realize you don't have "snow days" in L.A., but you must experience a day off from time to time. How do you spend it, and how does it feel to stop the routine and ignore your calendar, phone and computer?

"Monday, Monday. Back to Work, Monday."

Today it snowed and snowed and I didn't wear boots. A really dumb move. The new snow was way over my shoes.

When I got home the property was snow-white and smooth, dappled by prints of deer, rabbit and someone I couldn't identify. Nature inspires.

While I was at work, Max phoned and said, "It's starting to freeze." Indeed the lake is sending up ice. The steam rises each day as the lake gives up its heat (relatively speaking). Rugged and cold and lonely and lovely.

Do you realize what you are missing living in L.A.?

"So Glad You Are a Child of Mine." (from the song "Child of Mine" with lyrics by Carole King)

I heard this song on NPR this morning and it brought back memories.

I always get teary remembering you as a little one. I think about how you felt in my arms, how you smelled when hugged, what your first sounds were like, how you moved as a toddler and giggled over everything, and how you kept time to music, perfect time.

Driving you to the university's childcare center, you'd swing your bottle to and fro listening to the Carpenters or Abba or *Finlandia*.

Always an individual, you began dressing yourself as soon as you could stand. "*I* do, Momma," was your mantra. As a toddler your outfits included beads, hats, gloves and fancy shoes. You paraded around the house, sometimes holding the family cat upside down!

No one like you, my dear, from the beginning.

"The Music in Her Heart She Bore, Long After it was Heard No More."

Tonight we attended a brass band concert. It was held in the Chapel of the College of St. Scholastica. The inspiring music was made more so by the knowledge that the group is composed of medical doctors who love to play their horns.

I don't remember ever being without music. I went from dance lessons to piano lessons to violin lessons to organ lessons and loved them all. Singing in trios and choruses and choirs helped define my life. When I am down, music changes my outlook. A minister friend once said he plays a favorite symphony CD when there is a traffic delay. He said he almost hates to have his travels go back to normal.

The saying at the top of this message was in my high school yearbook under my photograph. What music lifts you up, Monette?

January 30, 2003

"Speaking Up"

My women's group met tonight. Connie, Sharon, Hommey and Pam are my dear friends of long standing. At first, it was all social and a discussion about illnesses and deaths, but I finally spoke up and asked, "What is one thing you would like to change about yourself?"

We sort of got around to answering it, but it was difficult. I am not sure why. (Maybe I asked because I am missing my NY therapy group.)

We will do better next time. But I did speak up, which is always difficult for me.

What is the one thing you would like to change about yourself?

"Live Simply"
"Free your heart from hatred.

Free your mind from worries.

Live simply.

Give more.

Expect less."

This was a message in my office mailbox today. I don't know who gave it to me or who wrote it, but it hit home.

What do you think of the quotation?

"Live simply" follows my Buddhist readings. I still don't do it, but I am thinking about it and what it would mean in my life. A friend in New York has taken this thinking to heart and absolutely rejects most "things" except for her paints and canvas. I so admire her.

The weather is warming. Cat Esme tells me each morning what the temperature is outdoors. Below zero, she won't go out. Above zero, she begs to do so. Guess I can throw out the thermometer, thus living more simply!

"WHITE RABBIT" (You got me.)

****

"Tragedy"

Today was a day of tragedy. We lost heroes in space. The space shuttle *Columbia*, with seven astronauts aboard, broke up when the "orbiter's damaged heat shield failed to protect it from the heat of re-entry as it attempted to enter earth's atmosphere." This is the third such tragedy that this country has endured.

You are old enough to remember the *Challenger* disaster in 1986. What do you remember and what were you told? You are not old enough to remember *Apollo 1* in 1967 when three astronauts died in a fire. There are risks in every field of endeavor, but the tragedies of space stay with us for a lifetime. They tell an important story of our country and speak of courage, bravery and inventiveness. My heart is so heavy today.

In response to today's *Columbia* tragedy, Max played the following to accompany my tears:

"Star Dust"
"How High the Moon"
"Blue Moon"
"Till the Clouds Roll By"
Can't write more. Too upset.

"Slow-Cooker Cassoulet" (I have no idea where I got this recipe but it is good.)

1/2 pound small white navy beans
lots of peeled and crushed garlic
1 large onion, chopped
3-5 carrots, peeled and cut into chunks
2 cups cored and chopped tomatoes with juice
4 sprigs of fresh thyme
3 bay leaves
1/4 pound bacon (I place on top and then remove before serving)
4 sweet Italian sausages, cooked and cut in smaller chunks
1 pound boneless pork shoulder
2 duck legs cooked (I sometimes skip)
Chicken stock (at the ready)

Combine beans, crushed garlic, onion, carrots, tomatoes, thyme, bay leaves and meats in slow cooker and turn heat to high. Add stock to cover the ingredients. Cover and cook until beans and meats are tender, 5 hours on high heat, 7 or more on low. I cut up the meat before serving. When done add salt and pepper to taste. If you like, you can remove the cassoulet from the slow-cooker and place in a deep casserole; cover with bread crumbs and roast at 400 degrees until bread crumbs brown, about 15 minutes. Garnish with fresh, chopped parsley.

Nice to have the day off to make cassoulet. Cleaned house, took a brisk walk followed by a long, hot bath, cooked, entertained and you called!

"Our View of the Viewing"

A friend's father died over the weekend and the "viewing" was today. My friend has watched her father's decline for months after his diagnosis of cancer. At the funeral home, there was a montage of photographs including reference to his career as a military man in WWII. A good funeral service.

It is a cold, snowy, blowing-hard, miserable winter day. People arrived in wool plaid shirts, car coats and parkas. They came to pay their respects in spite of the weather. It is the right thing to do.

After viewing the deceased in an open casket, friend Lucy and I turned to each other and said, "Cremation!"

"My Favorite Headshot"

     While driving to the airport this morning, we spoke about death. Max said the body is merely the "container of our soul." He believes the soul clearly separates from the body and goes to an "agreeable place." It is difficult for me to get him to focus on what he wants done when he dies. I am trying to figure this out for myself also.

     Is this too grim to write about and share with you? I hope not.

"Book It"

The book our club just read was *Aman: Story of a Somali Girl*. It is a heart-wrenching account told in the first-person by a young woman who was circumcised at 9 years of age, was the bride in an arranged marriage at 13, and who struggled between family tradition and freedom for women. This book invoked a spirited discussion about the role of the USA when it comes to our judgment, intentions and interventions with other countries like Somalia.

You may not recall that Peter and I visited Somalia when you were a little girl. I remember the beautiful people and the terrible difficulties they faced. Peter's parents met in Mogadishu (then the Italian Somaliland) and he wanted to experience the country. Years before, Peter's mother Giulia lived in Mogadishu, where her father was a third-ranking Italian diplomat. Peter's father Lawrence traded in furs and hides out of England, and he was hired by Giulia's family to give her piano lessons. Between etudes they fell in love and went on safari for their honeymoon.

Our monthly book club has in it the most amazing women. We have been reading books and discussing them together for years and years. We have all traveled the world and share the love of reading. I end up reading books I never would have selected myself, so it is an educational journey as well.

What are you reading? Have you ever thought about forming a book club? Does L.A. have such?

"Every Journey Begins with the First Step" (to paraphrase Lao-Tzu)

Max didn't want to go to NY this week. Lots of excuses and reasons to stay put. He had received an invitation to a reunion of Eubie Blake's friends. He was going to miss it.

But I pushed him and he went. He attended the dinner party and now has new interested parties for his own Mr. Dooley/Dunne musical, *Trust Everyone but Cut the Cards*. Hoorah! And his backer is meeting with him tomorrow. If he had remained in Northern Minnesota, he would have missed out.

Starting down a path means you're on your way. Love to you, my Pathfinder.

"You, the Actress, and Great-Aunt Fanny"

Ever wonder where your Thespian talent might have come from?

I believe it came from Fanny Niemi Pesonen. Better known in the family as Aunt Fanny. She was an amazing Finnish American woman...outgoing, huge smile, talented, had colorful shawls on tables, bowls of candy and hugged each of us like there was no tomorrow. Her life held drama and some mystery. She performed on stage in Minnesota, the region and NY. She was my grandmother's sister. Although Fanny's exuberance for life was a lot for me, an introvert, to take in, I loved her and was inspired by her. By the way, Aunt Effie knows a lot more about Fanny.

Grandma Johnson's other sister, Ina, had a son Ray Karkkinen. Ray's parents died and he was left to fend for himself at a young age. He was close to his Aunt Fanny and because of her influence, no doubt, Ray majored in theatre at UMD. He was a wonderful actor and moved to Hollywood where he worked. There is a seat named in memory of Ray at UMD's Marshall Performing Arts Center.

So maybe, just maybe, Aunt Fanny and Cousin Ray are watching over you, the actress, and shouting "Bravo" each time you enter the stage.

February 8, 2003

"When You Spin Out of Control, Try to Land Somewhere Soft."

Yes, today on the way to Ely, I spun out of control and friend Sharon and I ended up in the snow-drifted ditch. It happened so quickly and yet was somehow in slow-mo. A couple of kind passers-by took pity and pushed us back on the road. Good luck was with us!

Around the next turn and hill were five deer in the middle of the road. I thank God my spin, one hill prior, did not involve those beautiful deer.

Think I'll slow down a bit in the car...and in life.

What is your speed, Mosie?

February 9, 2003

"This One Really Works"

Have I ever told you that good people lead you to good people? This idea got played out when we moved from St. Paul, Minnesota to Columbia, Missouri. Eight northern friends gave me the names of folks "you simply must meet." I took down the coordinates of the referrals and brought them with me.

After unpacking I went through the list one-by-one and contacted and met each person. Voila! From this exercise I met Finnish professors, my next boss (President Patsy H. Sampson at Stephens College), a good friend for you, and a friend for me to walk with in the morning hours.

There was a ninth person in Minnesota, whom I did not care for, but who gave me a name to meet. I tried it and the new person was not someone I trusted and the meeting went nowhere.

This probably seems like an obvious exercise but it is not. When you move to a new city and know no one, it is much easier to just meet people by chance and let nature take its course. It seems a bother to call strangers and to set up a meeting.

But I tell you it works and is worth the effort.

Good night, Chickadee.

February 10, 2003

"Partnerships"

I have had wonderful working partnerships. Am thinking of Jane, when we served as co-directors of the Minneapolis Council of Camp Fire; Marianne and Carl, when we planned the two Finnish "Reunion of Sisters" conferences; Lucy and Jan, when we co-edited Pastor Jan's book; Max, when we created a book together; Libby, when we co-chaired with Rose the "Women of Ragtime" festival; Joan, as we co-edited our book on the president's spouse; and Chancellor and Maryann, as we travel the country together to bring the good news from the University of Minnesota Duluth (UMD) to alumni and donors. There is energy between people that is not possible alone.

I am wondering what it is like for you as an actress? You certainly depend on the work of others, your chemistry together, and the audience. Hard to act alone.

DIANE FAY SKOMARS

"Lead with Your Heart"

This is the week of hearts and flowers! It seems we are all a little kinder during this time that honors Valentines. We need reminders of our humanity. It is so easy to get hard in this life and forget our softer side.

Following one's heart instead of just one's head is rather risky but worth it. Nana always said the opposite. So, of course, I followed my heart. With such an innate urging, I have led a rather interesting life.

Where has your heart led you, my dear?

"Alone with Fear"

You called tonight from D.C. You had watched CNN and they painted a tough picture about our safety and security. You reported that the news anchor actually said we need to prepare for nuclear war. How sad that you are alone with such a message. I am sorry you are fearful of the future. I could hear in your voice how alone you felt and how frightened.

Before 9/11 we figured "never, never, us."

Now, we know better. So your fear is real. There are no guarantees that nothing will happen. All I know for sure is that you are not alone and you are loved.

February 13, 2003

"Facing Fear."

You are right. I just read the *New York Times* depicting Washington D.C. as having anti-missile aircraft launchers near where you are. D.C. is protecting its symbols and its people.

Perhaps it is best to just speak the truths:

1. The USA does seem fearful.
2. Osama bin Laden is still alive.
3. North Korea can aim its missiles at us and our friends.
4. Iraq doesn't plan to show its weapons of mass destruction.

Sometimes it helps to look at the map of the world and study where the key players come from, their neighbors, their history, their threats. Study can lead us to a better understanding of the world and, therefore, ourselves. It also provides an action step to take instead of just quaking in our boots.

There are many democracies in the world, but I am partial to ours. It is based on certain guaranteed freedoms and the right to vote for our elected officials, and the balance of powers. Our strength seems to lie in our resolve to do the right thing. Debate, real debate, is a key to our democracy because it allows for learned experts to share their insights and conclusions based on their fact finding, and allows us to decide which is the better answer.

I know 9/11 weighs on you, on me, on all of us. We will always be a threat to those who are extremists because they cannot fathom our kind of democracy and freedom of expression. I would like to believe we make the world a better place just by our very existence. And God bless those who defend our freedoms. I honor them and admire their courage.

"An Excuse to Express Love"

Your valentine was so special. You sent a card that said "I am always with you." How beautifully written. Thank you!

It pleases me that you celebrate "holidays" and times of commemoration. They spark up an ordinary day. These significant dates give us a reason to reach out to another...very important.

When I was in grade school, we decorated Cheerio boxes with construction paper of pink or red or white and attached hearts made out of doilies. We wrote our name on our box and HOPED to receive a valentine from that one special someone. Sometimes yes, sometimes no.

Thank you for having such a good heart and for sharing it.

"A Surprise"

Maxie surprised me on Valentine's Day with a black teddy bear sporting a bright red bow tie. I just love him! My friends at work wondered what the gift was in such a big box. We had fun guessing.

Whenever I am really down at work, I send myself flowers with a card enclosure that reads: "Remembering our time together at The Breakers..." It perks me up and keeps the staff wondering. What do you do to make yourself smile?

"Side by Side"

Max and I bought piano duet music in Minneapolis recently and came home and began to sight read it. It was such fun to sit side-by-side and play some familiar melodies and themes. In order to experience both the bass and soprano parts, we switched places.

Grandpa John Johnson once told Nana, "Marriage is like a team of horses, each one pulling his weight. Neither must get ahead of the other."

So it is written for musical duets and life.

Have you found it so?

"*The Hours*"

What a terrific film: complex, tragic, a certain sweetness, brave with multiple themes. In Virginia Woolf's day, a woman of letters could write about what was killing her, but she could not easily change her life - especially since she was ill. However, in 1951 Mrs. Brown couldn't write or talk about what was killing her - so she left her babies and husband. And in 2001 Meryl Streep could talk about what was killing her, and that saved her.

The dilemma of women has always been how not to lose **self** amidst serving others at home, at work and in the community. We are the doers, the re-actors, the caregivers...the ones who see the child in trouble, the animal in pain and the neighbor with problems. We sense when the world is unbalanced and we become the navigator to safety. We recognize false words, false people, false gods, false praise and just plain dishonesty. We are a gender of strength and wisdom and hard work. We rarely sit down.

From the beginning we are taught it is better to give than to receive and we do it in spades. We try to create a home that is a safe harbor from the outside. We cook, scrub, wash clothes, change beds, clean, organize car pools, pay bills, and shop. We shop to escape the ordinary and to find orderliness in stacks of colorful and pretty things. We also shop to find the best quality item at 75% off. We are the ones who send birthday cards to everyone we love without ever expecting anything back.

At work we are the peacemakers, the counselors, the pot-luck-lunch organizers, the early-to-arrive-workers and the ones who stay late. We help our bosses by putting out fires early, preparing reports based on truth, and by interpreting their intentions to others. We care deeply about the organization's goals or we move on.

After all of this, what is left of our time, resources, energy and creativity? Where is the **self**? Especially since on top of all that we do and give, we are supposed to look good!!!

I don't think I have ever talked to you about all this before, have I?

"10th Anniversary"

No matter what I say, the Max does not want a 10th anniversary party in May. I have tried everything, but no go.

The other day, I heard a wonderful recording of Max's "The Brass Ring." It is a joyous composition. So my latest idea is to get 50 CD's of his composition and send them out as our celebration. I doubt if he will buy it.

As my New York therapist always said, "Women want celebrations. Men want kisses."

Have you found this to be true, Monette?

February 19, 2003

"My Dear Mrs. Skomars"

I am watching *West Wing.* Yesterday my friend told me she wished Martin Sheen was the president our country because he is smart and sensitive and articulate as well as humorous, philosophical and thoughtful.

How did you arrive at your politics, my dear? As you know, I rarely followed Nana's advice, but I did follow Nana's politics. She was the Democrat and Pops the Republican.

When Nana was living alone and in the early stages of Alzheimer's, she was very worried about all the mail she was receiving from both political campaigns. She told me she wanted President Bill Clinton to know she could only send him a little bit of money. I told her to put all those letters in a shoebox and we would go over them when I next visited her. And we did just that, except there were two filled boxes. I was absolutely blown away by the number of mailings from both parties, tailor-made for the elderly, requesting donations. Because of the tone and the sense of urgency and the sheer number of mailings, they actually disgusted me. I could understand why Nana was worried about them and fearful of the possible consequences if she didn't respond.

She ended up writing a note to First Lady Hillary Clinton who had suggested Nana send President Bill Clinton a birthday card with a check for his campaign. In it Nana wrote that she was not able to contribute at this time. And we threw out the boxes of letters to "My Dear Mrs. Skomars..."

DIANE FAY SKOMARS

"Bachelorette"

As our relative came out of major surgery, he pulled out all the tubes and straps and sat up and said, "I'm out of here! I'm going home to watch the *Bachelorette.*"

I had lunch today with a woman friend. As we parted, she said, "Don't forget to watch the *Bachelorette.*'" Same thing happened with a colleague.

I believe everyone watched that show but me! Looks like most folks believe in romance. Do you?

"It's Schnowing"

It finally snowed here - inches and inches of the white stuff. And ours is here to stay. The irony this year is that you, in Washington D.C., had more snow in one storm than we have had all year.

It is so soft looking outside, so beautiful and calm.

Tonight, driving home from our friend's, we saw three car accidents and Max spun out twice! Guess we're going to have to get snow tires. We have been away from Minnesota for five years and simply forgot.

"Always be prepared," Nana said.

"Single Tracks in the Snow"

There are single tracks in the freshly fallen snow this morning. Like this:

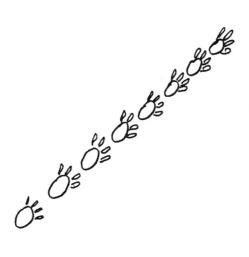

What in God's creation walks like this?

"Mexican Beef Stew" (from our wonderful friend Marilyn who was a life saver to me, and who helped me make table-cloths for events at Eastcliff)

> two pounds beef chunks (good cut)
> 1 can whole tomatoes
> 1 cup frozen whole onions
> 1 teaspoon chili powder
> 1 envelope taco seasoning mix
> 1 can black beans
> 1 can whole kernel corn (with red and green)

Mix beef chunks, tomatoes, frozen onions, chili powder into slow cooker.

Cover and cook on low heat for at least 9 hours until beef is tender. (Do not take cover off until you believe it is done cooking.)

Stir in taco seasoning mix using wire whisk. Stir in black beans and corn.

Cover and cook on high heat setting for 15-30 minutes. 6 servings. Yum!

Add a dab of sour cream or cheese on top and serve over rice or mashed potatoes or with taco chips.

****

By the way, I learned to measure a recipe by the following:

1. Make sure no item called for in the recipe is one you hate, or else that is all you will taste. I learned this from Marge.
2. The ingredients should consist mostly of real food, not processed ones.

3. When the recipe says, "20 minutes to prepare," double it.
4. People laughed at slow cookers, but for a working person inside and outside the home, they are great.
5. As you have told me, "Eat something green at every meal." In this case I would add a fresh green salad.
6. Add garlic cloves to everything possible. You will fall asleep with that heavenly fragrance on your hands.

February 24, 2003

"The Fall from Winter"

In the dark on my way from the garage to the cottage (12 degrees below zero), I fell on the ice. Not just "slipped," but FELL! My legs shot straight out and I hit my back and head. I cried and wailed. My papers (Student Worker of the Year Award nominee forms I had to read tonight) flew across the driveway. The wind was knocked out of me and I was scared. Was anything broken?

No, just my dignity, confidence and usual demeanor. I was shook up, sore and miserable.

I swore at winter. "I've had it, you &%@#*&!" I hobbled in and Max held me. I took Advil, took a hot bath, exercised to keep going, and took to bed.

Falls happen. Do you ever feel like giving up? How do you recover?

"Static Electricity"

This long, cold winter is fraught with obstacles. Get this!

After an especially tough day of work for me at the university, Max drove in from the shore and we ran errands and then planned on dinner out and a concert at UMD. We ran to Home Depot, Target, Lens Crafters, and TJ Max.

When I was in TJ Max, I tried on four hats. My hair stood on end and would not come down because of static electricity.

I felt so miserable and looked so awful, we drove home instead and ate leftovers, watched a movie and went to bed.

Have you ever been done in by static electricity?

February 26, 2003

"Do You Know What a WASP Is?"

Today I had such a thrill!

My friend Jerry in D.C. sent me an email urging me to look you up on the Arena Stage web site. There you were - in the cast of an Arena production. WOW! You looked great.

Jerry and I went to UMD together and were in an organization called "The Panel of Americans" (mixture of religions, genders, races). I was the WASP. Do you know what a WASP is? You will meet Jerry and Cynthia because they plan to see your play. They are special people.

You don't have to perform for me in order for me to feel pride. But I am so happy you are working at what you love.

I send you love today and all days.

"Dear Deer"

 While putting out some food for the stray cats in the neighborhood last night, three deer gazed at me, not in fear, but in curiosity.

 We watched each other, just a few yards away. I spoke softly to them and called them "darlings" and the two young ones grazing, slowly moved on.

 The doe lingered...and still we watched each other
ever mindful
of our sharing
of the earth,
and envious, perhaps, of the other.
Most lessons in life can be learned out-of-doors.

February 28, 2003

"Your Opening"

You said the flowers we sent were lovely. I am pleased. The florist who handled your order was so kind. She was as excited about your play as I was, and she plans to attend.

She even called me back to report who at the Arena Stage received the bouquet, and that she guaranteed you would love them. Now that is service! It's called Capitol Florist, if you ever need one.

This is YOUR night! At dinner we toasted you on the dot of your opening curtain.

How was it for you?

"WHITE RABBIT!" Got you!

****

"Once a Day"

Today someone told me they try to help one person each day.

This is doable and makes each day better.

Try it!

March 2, 2003

"Peace"

Today I made peace with someone I have held at bay for a long time. He sometimes made me uncomfortable with hurtful humor and jabs at what I hold dear. This time I let him know I care about him, just as he is, and he opened up like a flower about his fears and background. It all makes sense now, and I think that nothing he can say in the future will be received in the same way. Taking the first step is a powerful move when changing the nature of a less than perfect relationship.

I pay a price for confrontation; I would rather have a root canal. When you are raised to be "nice," you simply step aside from discord and do not fuss. But this time it felt good.

How do you handle people who make you uncomfortable?

"Accept Everyone"

Tonight we had dinner with neighbors, and looking across the restaurant, I recognized a friend from childhood. This friend came from a good family who were non-believers, according to Nana. "Don't talk about God," she told me at their doorstep. We all liked their company and it was never an issue. Once these same good people took me in when I got caught across town in a bad snowstorm. I have never forgotten their kindness. Although I have always been a believer in God, I learned early that one's religious and spiritual beliefs (or lack thereof) are private and there are good people and not-so-good in both camps.

Do you have friends of many faiths and friends who reject all religions?

What have you learned from them and what do you believe?

March 4, 2003

"Lapse into the Past"

Up at 4:30 a.m. to catch a plane to Minneapolis/St. Paul and on to Tucson. Nice to find the warm Arizona sun. We are here to remind alumni and donors about their connection to UMD and to thank them for their support. Development/fundraising is joyful work because people want to give back. It is less about asking for money than it is about honoring the donors, discovering who or what inspired them during their university days and bringing them up to date about the campus.

This evening the professional became personal when I had dinner with former university administrators and faculty. Bob reminded me that he and my dad, Pops, used to car pool to work, and occasionally I, as a wee girl, sat on Bob's lap as Pops drove. It was so special to hear about my dad from someone who knew and admired him.

As I say, my job is made easier because I am a Duluth native who also graduated from UMD and am now in its employ. I love the place.

The lesson? I believe one can only sell what one truly believes in.

DIANE FAY SKOMARS

"Waiting at the Wrong Restaurant"

Tucson still. Bad moment. I was supposed to meet an alum at a restaurant which I located but found it was closed for business. I called the alum several times but couldn't reach him. I waited around 45 minutes and then headed back to the hotel. I found out later the restaurant had moved a block away, and if I had just looked harder, I would have found it. Also I used the directions from the hotel and not from the alum himself. Big mistake.

This has never happened before. Feel so dumb. He was kind. I was awake half the night with night demons or as Max calls them, "the chattering monkeys." Do you know about them?

They whisper bad things in your ears when you are just falling asleep. The only way to combat them is to say, "You hold no power over me, You Chattering Monkey."* I have forgiven myself so you can vanish." Usually works. If not, rise and knit a scarf.

*One can use stronger names.

"A Toast to a Secretary"

Tonight Maryann and I had dinner with two women in their eighties. One worked as a secretary at the university for almost 30 years, where her husband was a janitor. She is now a significant donor to UMD thanks to Maryann. Some of the most generous people we know have wealth and don't show it. It is a special privilege to work with them.

Her friend had just flown in from Duluth to celebrate her 84th birthday. There was cake, music and celebration all around. At 84 I want to be a donor who celebrates! Love my job.

"You're Happy"

You're working...you're happy!

Your voice says it all! You are indeed happier when working at what you love. Being an actress is a high/low proposition: high when there is work and low when not so. I am glad you also have your successful jewelry business and are smart to take acting classes between gigs.

I am proud of you because you are working your dream. You will always act because you are talented with a strong work ethic and because you are relentless and never, never, never give up.

I hope *you* recognize your joy when you are rehearsing and on stage.

March 8, 2003

"My Most Romantic Moment"

In 1964, at age 21, I crossed the Atlantic with Nana, aboard the original *Queen Elizabeth*. The idea for this journey began when I told Nana we needed to visit our relatives in Finland. We were joined later by Aunt Effie and Cousin Sharon and together we four toured most of Europe and the Nordic Countries and had a ball! Effie and Sharon were wonderful traveling companions. Fortunately Nana would not fly at the time, so we were forced to sail. Thus began my love affair with the Cunard Line and travel.

Aboard the *Queen*, Nana did her thing (bridge and lectures and shows), and I was free to stay up all night and dance and hang out with girlfriends from England, USA, and Canada. By befriending the waiters and officers, we often snuck into First Class to dance. We gals had a drink with actor Victor Mature. He was a gentleman and he paid for the drinks.

But romance came when George, a singer from South Africa, sang "Fly Me to the Moon" just for me, under a full moon on the bow of the *Queen Elizabeth*. It was magic.

What has been your most romantic moment, Monette?

P.S. Just came across this poem written by cousin Sharon (pre-teen) at the end of the trip:

"One big, two big, three big man friends,
George, Jerry, Richard and little Ivan.
Hal, Mike, David and other man friends
All had adventure with lucky Diane."
You can see why I enjoyed the journey!

"On Dancing"

I love to dance, but I rarely do so.

Years ago at a conference in Finland with my friend Marianne, we returned to our hotel after a group dinner. Just as we entered the lobby, we heard live tango music and followed it.

A group of men from a hardware convention were enjoying the music. Remembering the old saying, "If you want to get to know a Finn, give him a drink and dance the tango," I sat and watched. Soon I was dancing with a hardware store owner from a small town and he danced my socks off. We never spoke and never sat down, dancing to every song. He was short and stocky and boy could he dance! We parted when the band stopped, never to learn the other's name and never to meet again. It was perfect.

Have you ever danced the night away?

March 10, 2003

"My First Airplane Ride"

Up at five a.m., I flew home today from Arizona. It took most of the day. At the airport I was searched up and down until they found what they were looking for: cuticle scissors!

Except for the search, the airplane ride reminded me of my first flight. When I was 19, Uncle Roy took me from Las Vegas to L.A. We flew at 6 a.m. over the Grand Canyon as the sun came up and the view was spectacular. I felt all grown up because someone asked Roy, "Who's your date?" "My niece," he said.

Your first flight was at age 6 months to California. By the time you were three years old, you had flown on twenty-three airplanes. And by the time you were six, you told *me* which line to enter at the airport and what gate to find.

I wonder if we will ever love air travel again?

"Flight of Faith"

Years ago in the Solomon Islands, seven of us from Stephens College flew with a bush pilot in a tiny plane from Guadalcanal to a small atoll. The aircraft was so small that I was the co-pilot.

Before departing, I observed the pilot in the hotel bar enjoying a lager and reading a manual on flying such a plane. No lie.

However, it turned out to be a terrific flight. Beautiful view of the sea with islands and atolls below. We saw the island where President Kennedy was rescued. Landing on a dirt path was high adventure. Loved it, loved it! This was probably my favorite flight. (Remind me to tell you more about this trip with Mary Josie, Dawn, Patsy and Jean and others.)

My least favorite was when you were a baby. We were flying home from a California Christmas with Nana and Pops, with a stop in Salt Lake City. The landing gear would not engage and we had to circle until the fuel was nearly gone. They foamed the runway and lined up the emergency vehicles. Just as we were about to land, the wheels dropped and we were saved from a tough spot. All I remember was holding you close and softly singing, "We Shall Overcome" in your tiny ear. I didn't want you to hear the people crying next to us.

"The Woman Takes a Drink. The Drink Takes a Drink. The Drink Takes the Woman." (to paraphrase Finley Peter Dunne's "Mr. Dooley")

I have never been comfortable around heavy drinking. I hate the way it changes some people. But drinking has two sides. One happy memory from childhood involving alcohol was Christmas Eve in my grandparents' log home with about 30 relatives. Grandpa Johnson would take out small glasses Nana had hand-painted and serve a bit of Mogen David wine all around. I can still taste the sweetness, see Uncle Martin dressed as Santa Claus, and hear Aunt Fanny leading Christmas carols. Loved my grandparents, aunts and uncles, and cousins, still do. And, although it is not hip to admit, I still prefer sweet wine.

The down side (with an upside) of drinking happened to me when Dan came with his team of Dallas firefighters to NYC after 9/11 and stopped at my studio of photography. Terrific guys! They visited fire stations, paid their respects to the first responders, attended funerals of fallen firefighters, and toured the city a bit. I photographed them and learned a lot.

Before they departed, we all ended up at "Suspenders," the famous bar near Ground Zero that reached out to the NYC firefighters and those from around the world who came to assist. I sat at the bar and heard the emotional singing of "God Bless America" from those brave men who filled the room with their rich voices. They also sent round after round of sweet drinks to "Aunt Diane." It was a memorable moment for me to be in the company of such a room full of bravery. I paid the price later, however, when I barely made it to the subway and back to my studio. Was sick all night from those innocent, sweet liqueurs on an empty stomach. Called you in the morning, and you said, "Momma, you have a hangover!"

How do you handle drink?

"A Woman's Work is Never Done."

    As I awoke this morning at 4 a.m. to do paper work and to pack for a trip to D.C. with Chancellor Kathryn, I was reminded of the phrase, "A woman's work is never done." Because your generation generally recognizes the worth of women and their contributions, you may have never read or heard it before.

    What the phrase means to me is that even if you run a tight ship at home (cleaning, cooking, child rearing and balancing the budget) and you put in the energy and hours at work to hold your job (being on time, achieving goals, getting along with everyone), there is yet another expectation. This one is the hidden one. Here are some examples:

1. You must call your mother today and every day because she looks forward to it and you need it. (15 minutes)
2. You won't sleep tonight unless you take the time to bring over the split pea soup you made to share it with your home-bound neighbor. (20 minutes)
3. You must listen to your husband's troubles on the road because he never complains but this time it sounds serious. (15 minutes)
4. Because her ear is bleeding, you must bring the cat to the vet. (45 minutes)
5. You must send your cousin a birthday card, your pastor a get-well card and write a note to your friend who had a big bump at work. (10 minutes)
6. You must get out the invitations for a reception you are planning with a friend. (45 minutes)
7. You must fix the dripping faucet, bake beer bread for the potluck at work, and plan to replace your worn out sheets. (60 minutes)

8.   And you must move your winter clothes to the other closet because you are sick to death of your woolens even though it will probably snow tomorrow! (20 minutes)

I write this hidden list of expectations, not as a complaint but with pride because women are the keepers of the details, the glue that holds it all together, and the heart that would truly rather give than receive.

March 14, 2003

"Bravo!"

After working all day, I saw you on stage tonight in D.C. I cannot believe how amazing you are on stage. Believable, consistent, talented, strong, compelling, engaging, interactive, attentive, fabulous!

Bravo, my darling daughter.

"D.C."

Washington D.C. brings back happy memories. Before you were born, your father and I lived here for nine months. Actually, in Rockwell, Maryland. Your father worked in the District and I volunteered at Georgetown's UN Shop, taught catechism at a local Lutheran church, and played tennis with my neighbor who, when introducing me to her husband said, "She's from one of the 'M' states."

That summer we had 14 sets of visitors (including my very special cousin, Lea, from Finland who didn't know it yet, but was on her way to Minnesota to meet her future husband David), and I arranged for tours of the White House and the Capitol Building, and I got to know and love the District.

Each weekend your father and I went on trips to such places as Monticello, NYC, Pennsylvania Dutch Country, Civil War battle-fields, the Atlantic Ocean, Appalachian Trail. A happy time.

Do you remember when you first visited our nation's capi-tal? I do. You were eight years old with pigtails. You liked everything you saw especially the Smithsonian Museum, Lincoln Memorial, Theodore Roosevelt Island and the National Museum of Art. And you loved the red/white/blue popsicles.

"New York, New York"

haveyoueverhadoneofthosetimeswhereyoutrytodoto-
omuchandthewholethingbackfiresinasenseldidittodaybytakingthet-
raintoNYCandbackandinfiveshorthourslsawfriendDonnaandhadlun-
chandattendedamuseumexhibitionthetrainrideupwasokaybutcom-
ingbacklhadtostandformostoftheridewhenlfinallygottositlsatnext-
toayoungwomanwhorepresentsherpianoperformerhusbanditturn-
soutshehadaboothnearourswhenwerepresentedMaxMorathattheA-
PACconventioninNYCattheHiltonlrememberyourpitchingMaxtovisi-
torstoourboothwehadalotofpeoplestopbybecauseofyouandyourener-
gyandpersuasivenessitwasloadsoffunyouprobablywonderwhylam-
writinglikethisitisbecauseitbestrepresentshowifeelaboutsuchadayin-
NYC

March 17, 2003

"War on St. Patrick's Day?"

We spent St. Patrick's Day together in our nation's capitol. A fun day of walking, shopping and dining. Our kind of day, my dear.

We woke up believing the war was about to start. We learned later that Iraq has "48 hours." Unless Congress and the President are willing to send their own sons and daughters and move in sync with the UN, we should not consider war. I wasn't a young adult in the 60s for nothing.

Have you ever talked to someone who was in active combat duty during a war? If not, make it a goal.

"Every Day I Say Out Loud..." (Psalm 23)

"The Lord is my shepherd, I shall not want;
he makes me to lie down in green pastures.
He leads me beside still waters;
he restores my soul.
He leads me in the path of righteousness
for his name's sake.
Even though I walk through the
valley of the shadow of death,
I fear no evil;
for thou art with me;
thy rod and thy staff,
 they comfort me.
Thou preparest a table before me
 in the presence of my enemies;
thou anointest my head with oil,
my cup overflows.
Surely goodness and mercy shall
follow me
all the days of my life;
and I shall dwell in the house of the
Lord
for ever...
And God bless Monette."

March 19, 2003

"The Stranger at the Table'

    I will forever remember our cab ride after dinner in D.C. hearing Alice Walker on the radio urging us to set a place at the table for the stranger at the door...

    and hearing that our troops dropped a bomb that killed a small boy

    and her urging us to set a place at the table for that small boy.

    You and I held hands in that taxi.

"I Can See the End"

I remember the day that Max said, "I can see the end." My heart was heavy and I told him, "You can't die, you're booked." When you reach the other side of sixty, things change. Time speeds up on the outside and memories grow deeper on the inside.

You accept the fact that you will never be rich, thin or powerful. You are simply glad for a job, a couple of people who love you, and a sense that there is a force greater than this earth and place. And yes, the body does change, shift and droop. Waves of wrinkles weave their way across the face and one stops going strapless or even sleeveless.

Accepting one's age is important and so is loving oneself just as we are, with all our failings and successes, warts and awards, sins and titles.

You are almost thirty. A wonderful age. Each decade brings good things. The decade of the twenties brings exploration, energy and excitement. The thirties focus on commitment, achievement, and a settling down. In the forties one asks the big question, "Why am I here?" and in the fifties, one answers it. And in the sixties you begin attending funerals of friends and know it is "now or never." If you are fortunate enough to have enough money and time, you can began exploring new interests and taking new journeys. By now one is grateful for every act of kindness and every day of breath.

I will let you know about the seventies when I get there. In the meantime, enjoy each decade!

March 21, 2003

"Women Score"

As I mentioned earlier, growing up, it was the girls who stood in the cold on the sidelines to cheer on the hockey player boys. Hockey in Duluth, Minnesota meant the guys skating to victory, and there was plenty of speed, fights, and bloodshed in the process.

There was a fever about ice hockey. As girls, we couldn't wait for the games, to wear the leather jacket of our favorite player, and to cheer until we lost our voices. We skipped school to go to the state championships in the Twin Cities and stayed in a hotel, six to a room. It was glorious. But always there was envy.

Envy of the guys who got to play, be in the spotlight and be adored by fans. We thought we were cool by cheering, but we knew the women athletes among us should be playing. One brave girl, Bonnie, used hockey skates and practiced with the boys and tried out for the team. High school administration said "No." Recently I saw Bonnie and was able to tell her she was always a hero to me. She skated for the love of the game and she had skill and determination. I remember watching her practice by herself, in the cold at the outdoor rinks and thinking, Bonnie knows something the rest of us don't.

If you live long enough there is justice. Tomorrow the UMD women play Harvard.

DIANE FAY SKOMARS

"Number One in the Nation"

Today UMD beat Harvard in Women's Hockey!!! They were 3 to 3 at the end of the game and UMD won in two overtimes. It was a great game.

Since we were quite evenly matched, I have pondered why we were so fortunate. Clearly our exceptional Coach Shannon, whom our Chancellor recruited from Canada, and our players made the difference. And we had the home ice advantage. But I think there was another reason.

The reason we won was because a national "win" in Duluth means more to us, than another "win" for Harvard. And because this win means Bonnie won...in the end.

Do you still have your skates?

"The Academy Awards"

Being raised up North and having enough of camping and boating and skating, I found the movies were a great escape for me. And to this day, I see one or two movies weekly and repeat the good ones at home.

With the dimming of the lights, popcorn in hand and the trailers over, I can escape into the cinematic story and forget my other life. I have only walked out on two movies, *Groundhog Day* and *A Clockwork Orange*. The first was too dumb and the second too manipulative.

So tonight is my night; the Academy Awards are on! You and I will call each other five times to dish on the dresses, awards, and speeches. We will also figure out who won the Oscar competition. Kathy won last year.

I am sorry to admit that the first movie you saw was *The Exorcist*. This doesn't count, however, because it was at an outdoor theatre in St. Paul and we lowered the sound and covered your tiny ears during the bad parts. The movie you loved the most was *New York, New York*. You clapped your hands and sang loudly from the back row.

You, my actress daughter, will some day really make it *in* the movies and not just *to* the movies.

"Time Out"

Tonight we had dinner with friends. I felt miserable! My earring broke so I had to take both out. The sweater I was wearing was wool and uncomfortable. My hair fell in the wind and hung in my eyes, not the neat way, the sad way. My pantyhose were tight and my stomach ached. And I was exhausted.

So when the waitress was soooo happy and cheery, I felt miserable. I watched myself grow smaller and smaller.

However, just before I "disappeared," I headed to the ladies' room and looked at myself in the mirror and said, "You are a worthy person and fun to be around." And I splashed cold water on my face, took off my pantyhose, and fluffed up my hair and rejoined the group. It felt better, not great, just better. I didn't go dark. My New York shrink taught me how to do it. Cripes! I hate this part of me. Feel dumb.

Do you ever have such hits?

"Slumber"

Sleep really helps. Last night I slept a full eight hours and today I feel good to go. And I know how you feel about sleep.

As a mother, I found it difficult to wake you for school each morning. You slept so deeply and looked like an angel in the morning light, still and peaceful, and you never wanted to get up. The dogs, Bandit and Molly, and our three-legged cat, Mouse, came into your room to lick your face awake, but sometimes even that didn't work.

Slowly you'd awaken if I stroked your nose like a pussycat. "Five more minutes, please," you'd beg and roll over. A lovely daughter in repose. My daughter.

Do you still love to sleep, sweet girl?

"When I Cannot Sleep"

When I simply cannot sleep, I determine why I cannot sleep. If it is because I am upset about something, I acknowledge it and...

1. Analyze it from all sides and put it in a box and divide the box in quarters.
2. Then I pull apart the quarters and let them float away in different directions,
3. I chant, "Let go; Let God" over and over.
4. Finally I say, "Rest is good and all I need," and I relax.

Try it!

"Borderline"

It is the end of March and we are having a blizzard! As friend Susan would say, "holy buckets!" What is really bad is, I like it!

Have to drive to Minneapolis/St. Paul tomorrow in the new snow. I really don't mind because it adds to the excitement of the day.

Fighting with nature puts one at risk in a way nothing "person-made" can. There is so little control.

Do you like a good storm? To stand in the rain buck-naked? To jump in a lake when the water is about 50 degrees? To roll in the snow after a sauna?

Of course not. Because you are sane and your mother is borderline.

"Friends"

I drove through snow and blizzard, met with donors, had meetings, and dined with an old friend. He has known you since you were but an infant. I brought photographs of you and he declared you "a beauty." He wanted to know all about you and he brought me up to date on his family.

He got me thinking about friends. There is a saying, "A thousand relatives don't equal one loyal friend." Well, friends are important but so are loyal relatives. If one is fortunate, one has both.

My definition of a friend is someone who loves you, just as you are, and knows how to keep things you tell her "in the vault." You believe a friend is someone who leaves you feeling better about yourself. Great definitions!

Looking back, you were always loyal to your friends. Now, at this time in your life, who are your friends?

March 29, 2003

"Guthrie Theatre"

Friend Claudia and I saw *Six Degrees of Separation* tonight at the Guthrie Theatre. It seems like I have been attending performances at the Guthrie all my life. Have especially loved the work of actor Peter Michael Goetz who has been a mainstay at the theatre. Anyhow, have you seen this play? It was wonderfully done.

The plot is based on a young man who pretends he is the son of a movie star and gains access to the apartment of an upper-class couple in NYC. You know the concept of "six degrees of separation." This is a complex play with a sad ending.

Whenever I see a play, television series, or film, I always recast the young woman lead with you in it. You do beautifully, of course.

What was the first live theatre production you remember seeing? Did you know then that you wanted to be on the stage?

March 30, 2003

"Fisk University"

Max is thinking about starting an endowed scholarship at Fisk University in Nashville in his name. He wants to give back to a campus that especially honors the contributions of African American musicians. I truly understand how important it is to support a cause you believe in. It changes your life because it is the right thing to do.

So we will get started!

Look them up: www.fisk.edu

March 31, 2003

"Max is Arriving!"

As you know, Max travels a lot and there are weeks of my life without him. I truly miss the Max at these intervals of absence. But today, he comes home! Therefore it is a good day. It is like carrying a secret inside.

All day I am happy because when work is done, I will drive to the Duluth International Airport to pick him up. And when he arrives, Max will be in a great mood and ask questions about my life and he will say, "I am glad to be home."

He is one in a million - smart, kind, funny. He is always changing names like, "Noble and Barnes" ("because Barnes shouldn't always get top billing"). Also "Dr. Chicago" for "*Dr. Zhivago.*" And "hamlet" for "omelet" and on and on. He has played over 5,000 concerts crisscrossing the USA in opera houses, theatres, high schools, synagogues, outdoor parks, ships, and of course NY venues. Max Morath has written books, music, and musicals. He has mentored dozens of musicians first telling them, "Don't go into show business unless your spouse is a dentist; there are bills to pay." Second, he advises, "Show business is as much about "business" as it is about "show." And finally, "Talent is everywhere; you must distinguish yourself and create a property." He is so much more than a Ragtime Entertainer. He actually reads the *NY Times, New Yorker, The Nation* cover to cover and can quote from each article. In his seventies, he received a master's degree from Columbia University in American Studies focusing on the work of Carrie Jacobs Bond who wrote "I Love You Truly." I am his biggest fan.

We met in 1964 in Kirby Ballroom at UMD where he was performing with his quartet. He pretends he remembers me, the blonde in the front row cheering loudly, but he doesn't. Through the years I heard him perform throughout the country often being featured at a campus where I worked. We became holiday-card-friends and had occasional lunches when we each paid. Our first real date was in NYC when he took me to see *Jelly's Last Jam* and to dinner at Joe Allen's. He paid. The rest is history, a lovely history. I hope for you, such a mate.

April 1, 2003

"White Rabbit" You got me!

****

"The Call"

You flew across the country and landed safely in California. Thanks for calling as we always do upon arrival.

You may not realize it, but your momma holds her breath all day when you are in the air.

It is my job to worry and your job to call me when you land.

"It is Difficult to Find Peace Through War"

War has somehow become inevitable, with the excuse, "War will lead to peace." Rarely possible. Unless we are directly attacked or can **prove** we are about to be attacked, we need to avoid it at all costs. Our President believes 9/11 was the beginning of a war. However, he must not link it to reasons to attack Iraq.

And once we attack and invade a country, we stay forever. We say it is in the name of security and promoting democracy, and yet when that country does vote for the first time and we don't like the outcome, we stay involved in **their** business.

Understanding and respecting other countries, cultures and religions is step number one to avoiding war. Those who have travelled the world, learned other languages, read widely about other cultures and religions are generally more opposed to war, I believe. I look for those kinds of experiences in every candidate I vote for when it comes to elections.

To get a perspective on the world, I urge you to go to Barnes and Noble and buy the latest world map (they change every year). Tape it to your wall and find the USA. What do you notice?

And make no mistake. I love my country with all my heart.

April 3, 2003

"April Showers, Indeed!"

Another sleet storm with 50 mph winds! A miserable day. A 1,000 foot ore boat got stuck in the Canal because of ice, wind and waves. We have had storm after storm this spring. Tough to take after we thought winter had vanished.

One morning my Toyota blasted through 15 inches of snow. Nothing was plowed and the winds caused major drifting. It was 6:30 a.m. and I was determined to get to work, and I made it! Churned up most of the gravel in the driveway. It was exciting.

I certainly have a "macho side." Do you?

DIANE FAY SKOMARS

"Sleep Cycle"

I slept eleven hours last night. How many hours of sleep do you need? I usually need seven hours (9:30 p.m. - 4:30 a.m.).

They say one cannot "catch up" on sleep. I've never learned who "they" are and I don't believe it is true. I will feel rested all week because of those eleven hours.

When I write these pages to you at night, sometimes I can hardly keep awake. I have always been a morning person. If it hasn't happened by noon, it's not going to happen for me.

I wonder what makes us morning people versus night people? Necessity, inner clocks, level of activity? All I know is the world is beautiful in the morning with the rising sun over the most superior Lake Superior and the early hours filled with promise for a new day.

Good night, Mosie.

April 5, 2003

"One Sentence"

"Three little fir trees teetering on the edge of the cliff above the great Lake Superior are draped with ice crystals weighting them down so heavily that they resemble three sisters wearing old ball gowns having lost their poof."

After writing this sentence last evening, I felt good because I pushed myself to write with more flourish. However, one good sentence does not a writer make. I like to push myself: to be a writer when I am not one; to get certified for scuba diving when afraid to go underwater; to take adventure trips that lead me way out of my comfort zone. Learning for me is 95% experiential. I simply don't trust what I read and hear from others. Must do it myself.

You seem to be more careful (or smarter) than I am when it comes to trying new things. Is this true?

April 6, 2003

"Have I Remembered to Tell You?"

1. When your eyelids are puffy, lean over the sink and put a very hot washcloth on your eye- lids until the cloth cools down. Repeat three times. Then rinse with ice water.
2. If your arms ache, sleep on your back with your arms crossed.
3. Back exercises every day prevent backaches. I can share my routine if you like.
4. Eat melons by themselves, not with other food.
5. Massage your gums every day. They are as important as your teeth.
6. "An apple a day keeps the doctor away."
7. The next time it rains, go onto your patio (at night!) and stand au natural. You will sleep like a baby.
8. Never have references to your work in your bedroom, or your sleep will be interrupted.
9. Stretch like a cat every morning.
10. Sing out loud every day of your life.
11. Wear your high, high heels only an hour a day.
12. If you ever own a new car, "key" it the first week and no future dents will bother you.
13. Be different, never swear.
14. Never use Wikipedia for anything.
15. Use the first stall in the public ladies room because others don't.

April 7, 2003

"Nana"

This is the birthday month of my mother,Toinie Sylvia (Johnson) Skomars, who was born and raised in Cedar Valley, Minnesota. The eldest of six siblings, my mom told me she worked hard growing up. There were potatoes to plant and peel, younger siblings to watch over, and farm hands to feed. Her escape was books and learning, and she loved school.

Finnish-Americans were considered clannish by some, at that time in their farming community. It had to be the language barrier. Unlike Swedish, the Finnish language is difficult to learn and to understand. Nana, therefore, learned the "King's English" and had perfect diction.

Toinie loved her parents, Hilja and John; brothers, Leo and Bruno, and Ralph who died at a young age; and she was especially close to her sisters, Effie and Fay. These three women made a big impact on me growing up, and made me wish I had a sister. Artistically talented, they could each tell a great story, and I loved to listen to them. Their beauty and poise stood out. They lapsed into Finnish when the story got interesting.

Nana was a painter, gardener, organizer, good public speaker, and crackerjack entertainer and housekeeper. Our home ran like clockwork: Nana baked bread and cookies and pies on Friday; Saturday we changed the sheets (the tops went to the bottoms) and cleaned; Sunday was church followed by a delicious meal of pot roast, mounds of potatoes and gravy especially for my brothers, canned beans, small salad, her bread slathered with Land O' Lakes Butter ("to support my brother Leo") and pie. Every morning we had oatmeal, and lunch was peanut butter and jelly (homemade crab apple jelly, thanks to Nana and a backyard tree) and chocolate chip cookies. I still dream of Nana's chocolate chip cookies.

DIANE FAY SKOMARS

Nana was a mother cat and took no prisoners. If you crossed her, she remembered it. She was protective of her family and gave us strong advice growing up. Once, when I was hurt by a girlfriend, she told me, "Go back to school smiling and befriend someone new and never give that girl the satisfaction of knowing she hurt you."

"Nana" continued...

Nana was famous for her Christmas Cranberry Crush laced with alcohol. It took her days to decorate her home for the holidays. You and I always looked forward to Nana "sewing, then lifting her lip" (her best pantomime). She was an artist who painted china figurines; tooled in leather to create wallets and purses and belts; sewed matching dresses for us until I put my foot down and demanded a dress from Wahl's Department Store for my sixth grade party.

I will be forever grateful to Nana for our trip to Europe when I was 21, with Aunt Effie and Cousin Sharon (15 countries in two months), and proud of her for moving to Tasmania, Australia with Pops for his job. But her finest hour was caring for Pops at the end of his life. Suffering a slow decline in health, Pops had emphysema and was on oxygen. He stayed home for as long as possible, and Nana was his caregiver, pill dispenser, cook and cleaning lady, schedule-keeper for medical appointments and home visits, and his cheerleader. She helped him in and out of bed and handled social visitors. She paid a big price for their decision to keep him in the house, and it was wrenching for them to decide to move him into a setting with 24-hour care. After Pop's death, Nana kept his shirts in their closet for a long time. She told me she loved to see them there and to touch and smell them. She also had each of us select a shirt or two to keep.

At the end she would only make right turns when she drove. "It's easier to turn right." (Don't ask!) I had taught her to drive when she was over 50 and she was very pleased to finally pass her driver's test on the third try.

Nana was a proud, talented, hard-working, good-looking woman. She was loyal to her family and friends and very, very smart. She cried when we came and cried when we left, and often said, "I feel like I'm in a dream" when having a good time.

Sweet dreams, my mother, our Nana.

"To Extend Your Life"
  You will live longer if you:

  1. Love
  2. Laugh
  3. Listen
  4. Learn
  5. Let go
  6. Lift your weight
  7. Lead by example
  8. Look for ways to help others

April 10, 2003

"70 Degrees Above!!!"

The ice is breaking up! The snow is melting! The winds have calmed and the sun is out!

Everyone feels renewed. No one deserves better weather than Northerners.

Students are in shorts. Faculty members have rolled up their sleeves. Esme begs to go out. Although I feel like tearing off my clothing to sunbathe, I will spare the neighborhood fox such a display of flesh.

April 11, 2003

"Mia and Monette"

You and your cousin Mia from Finland celebrated your first and second birthdays together and have visited each other five times. Here is my favorite photograph of you two as women. You have much in common besides your beauty: you both are artists, animal lovers, and independent. Family has brought you together. I hope you always stay in close touch.

April 12, 2003

"Our Easter Lily"

Easter for me meant wearing a homemade dress with a coat featuring the same flowered dress fabric in the coat's lining, a straw hat with streamers cascading down the back, and new black patent leather shoes from Bakers. And it often meant snow, and snow meant sitting in church attentive to Pastor Wellington's sermon, with wet shoes and a drooping hat that, as the snow melted, dripped large drops onto the pages of the hymnal. As Nana said, "It's hard to be glamorous in Duluth."

Do you remember we always had hot cross buns and a lily plant at Easter and you had a new dress for church? They are excellent reminders of spring. The fragrance and delicacy of the lily are such a sharp contrast next to the remnants of the spent winter.

DIANE FAY SKOMARS

April 13, 2003

"Child Care"

Because there was no choice and because there was excellent childcare available for you as both an infant and toddler, you were watched first by our dear neighbor Bonnie by day, and later at the University of Minnesota Twin Cities Child Care Center.

I will never forget the first time I brought you to the center. I helped you hang up your jacket and hat, and off you ran to play with new friends. Not once did you cry and not once did you wave good-bye. You loved your new home and knew your momma would be there at the end of the day. Susan was your favorite teacher and Batala your best friend. Because you were an only child, I was grateful for this safe, stimulating, loving place that taught you about sharing and friendship. I believe a child deserves to have peers around and many good, adult role models.

Each day in the car we sang, "We are off to work today. We are off to work today." I told you your job was to learn something important each day and to get along with others. You gave me a full report as we drove home until you fell asleep in your car seat, happy and tired.

Did I ever mention that I marched for childcare in front of Northrup Auditorium at the University of Minnesota Twin Cities? I was pregnant with you at the time so this was your first public march.

The concept of "child care" outside the home has always triggered a strong response from the public. What are your feelings on the subject?

"Have I Taught You How to Grieve With Others?"

When I was a kid, a young child in our neighborhood fell from a cliff in Duluth and died. (This cliff was the same one my friend Judith and I had climbed many times to look down on our neighborhood and plan our lives.) I remember that Nana packed up a loaf of homemade bread and a jar of crab apple jelly. She took my hand and we visited the family in mourning. I watched Nana as she expressed words of comfort, listened to the story of the fall, cried with the mother, and gave those homemade gifts.

Years later, we visited Aunt Fanny who was dying in the hospital. Eyes closed, unable to speak, Fanny lay perfectly still. Nana brought flowers in a vase, spoke to Fanny in Finnish, and we sang to her and sat with her. Nana held Fanny's hand throughout our visit. She kissed her aunt's cheek and we departed. Once we were in the hallway Nana told me, "Always remember, hearing goes last. Assume the person can hear you until her last breath."

Then Nana told me a story from her mother. When Nana's mother, your great Grandmother Hilja, was very, very ill and was in bed for days, a neighbor came by and insisted on putting pennies on my grandmother's closed eyes to show grandmother had died. Grandmother claimed she heard it and came back to life to prove the woman wrong!

"Tax Day"

I never mind paying taxes because they support:

military
public restrooms
roads
Amtrak
welfare
Social Security
Head Start
schools
kids' lunches
health clinics
FBI
Peace Corps
D.C. monuments
Park Services
Department of Interior
Supreme Court
Congress
Post Office
NPR
research
National Endowment for the Arts
National Institute of Health
student aid
libraries

How do you feel about paying taxes?

April 16, 2003

"I'll Take Care of Your Cares for You"

"I'll take care of your cares for you.
I'll be there when you're feeling blue.
Let me be your one ray of sunshine.
Maybe you'll remember somewhere, sometime.
I won't scold you for your mistakes,
I'll just hold you when your heart aches.
Keep me in your thoughts, your dreams, and your prayers,
And I'll take care of your cares."

A lovely song Max and I often sing to each other, and today it is dedicated to you.
By Mort Dickson and James Monaco 1927
Revived by Frankie Lane 1967

DIANE FAY SKOMARS

April 17, 2003

"My Presidents"

Franklin Delano Roosevelt
Harry S. Truman
Dwight D. Eisenhower
John F. Kennedy
Lyndon B. Johnson
Richard Nixon
Gerald Ford
Jimmy Carter
Ronald Reagan
George Bush
Bill Clinton
George W. Bush

These are all my presidents, to date in 2003, in my lifetime. It is a terrible job, so I salute each one and his mate. I have always hoped that the Presidents who are alive have formed a secret pact, a private club, which meets from time-to-time to advise and support the current place-holder. Too much burden to carry alone.

April 18, 2003

"At the Ready"

Henry A. Wallace/Harry S Truman
Alben Barkley
Richard Nixon
Lyndon B. Johnson
Hubert Humphrey*
Spiro Agnew/Gerald Ford
Nelson Rockefeller
Walter Mondale* (He is the best!)
George Bush
Dan Quayle
Al Gore
Dick Cheney

These are all the Vice Presidents in my lifetime, to date. I have included them in order to list two outstanding Minnesotans! (*)

I love what Finley Peter Dunne's "Mr. Dooley" wrote about the Vice President: ... "He has to be an all-around man. A good speaker, a pleasant man with the ladies, a fair boxer and wrestler, something of a liar, and if he's a Republican campaignin' in Texas, an active sprinter.

Every morning it is his business to call at the White House and inquire after the president's health. When told that the president was never better, he gives three cheers and departs with a heavy heart.

It is principally because of the vice-presidents that most of our presidents have enjoyed such rugged health. The president, after sizing up the vice-president, concludes that it would be better for the country if he should live yet a while."...

From time to time, it is good to put yourself in a historical context. You are a person born of a larger history, as well as from a personal journey. For example the summer you were born was the summer of the Watergate Trials...the President of the USA was being asked to step down because of bad deeds. Did you study the downfall of President Nixon in school? What did you learn?

"Errands"

> Pick up the Max at the airport
> Go see the film *Holes*
> Eat lunch out
> Pick up lotion at drug store
> Buy groceries
> Purchase gas
> Recycle
> Visit Pam and Neale
> Visit Bob and Hommey
> Visit Milton and bring a lily plant
> Wash clothes
> Feed Esme
> Bake a pie
> Take a bath
> What does it all add up to?

It is easy to get lost in the errands and forget to take time to breathe!

"Easter Sunday"

I have always loved Easter! Sign of spring. Today the weather is bleak and rainy but it still smells of spring.

Wet earth, brave first robins on the hunt for sluggish worms, return of the seagulls squawking for my bread crumbs, long walks without a hat, car finally unplugged from the winter, tiniest buds on the tree not yet green but hopeful, the earth now brown instead of white, 90% of ice off the lake, first fishing boat on the big lake with guy dressed in a parka, smelt on the run in the rivers and offered in restaurants, asparagus in the stores, hot cross buns for sale, snow boots moved to the back of the closest.

It's Spring here in the North. I love this time of year! How do you know it is Spring in L.A.?

April 21, 2003

"Sheldon"

Is he always so calm?

Do you see that he has the face of an angel and the voice
of God?

Isn't it great that you can count on him to be there for you?

You share the theatre, the perfect house, and love.

You seem to compliment each other.

Nice to have a partner who is grounded

Lucky you. Lucky him.

"We Never Really Own Anything, So Why Not Give It Away?"

In 1998 our university capital campaign was set at $28,000,000. Because of the generosity of donors, the leadership at UMD and an amazing staff, we reached $36,000,000. Thank goodness Chancellor Kathryn believes in development and is an exceptional fundraiser.

I am frequently asked about fund raising: "I could never ask for money. How do you do it?" Fund raising is like any other profession. Here are the guidelines: 1. Know what you are representing. 2. Believe in your institution. 3. Build a relationship with your alumni and potential donors. 4. Listen to them. 5. Tell the university story. 6. Receive the gift and thank them. 7. Steward the gift properly. Number four is the most neglected in my profession. Development is NEVER about you, the fundraiser. It is always about the donor.

Because people want to do the right thing, you rarely have to ask for gifts. Your role is to *help them* do so when they are ready. Some of the most satisfying moments in my career have occurred when a donor was matched with the needs of the university at just the right time. And some of the most generous people I have met are those who live simply and give most away.

God bless the donors who have learned how to share. And God bless you, Monette, for your donations to your selected charities.

April 23, 2003

"The Three Block Rule"

You taught me this rule, remember? It goes like this:

When you attend a cultural event (play, film, musical, lecture, ballet, symphony concert, jazz night, opera), never discuss it with another person until you are three blocks away. That way you can digest what you have seen and heard, form your own opinion, and get some distance before someone else presents his/her views.

How many times have you *loved* a movie only to have your partner say, "Well, that was horrible!" The three block rule gives you time to sort out your own thoughts before someone puts a damper on it. And *you* can't rain on someone else's parade.

The other reason to wait before verbalizing judgment is because someone connected to the production might overhear your remarks and take them to heart without your knowing it.

"Drum Song"

There are few experiences that have the power to transport you to an ancient calling, but I promise you, hearing an American Indian Drum song can do just that. This Saturday is an American Indian Powwow at the university. There will be dance, song and a social atmosphere, but it will be the Drum Song, performed mostly by young men, that will open my heart.

Since the time Chancellor Martin was inaugurated, she has included the Drum Song at commencement and other important events at UMD. The drummers/singers invoke the spirit world and lift us to see beyond the here and now. It is an amazing gift they have.

This year's theme is a call to learn the Ojibwa (Anishinabe) language, which puts one on a spiritual journey. The elders in this area are beginning the task and joy of teaching the children the language. Learning their own language is a tribute to the past and a promise for the future.

There has always been a close connection between Finnish Americans and American Indians. Perhaps it is because both have difficult languages and both are sometimes considered clannish. I believe they share the love of nature, belief in the four seasons to teach basic truths, and they respect each other's culture. Friends George and Rick have taught me the most about Indian ways and I am grateful to them.

I urge you to attend an Indian Powwow. You will never, ever, forget it.

April 25, 2003

"End Days"

Our friend, Bob, is very much on our mind because he just learned he has terminal cancer. A tough time for him and for his family. He is at home.

From what I know, it is best for a dying person to have someone help them go over - hopefully, someone they love, who says it is okay. But that is not always possible. No worries either way. What is important is that each of us is in a "right relationship" with our loved ones.

Our end days seem like an exaggeration of who we are. Angry people seem to die angry. Lonely people die lonely. Engaged people are still worrying about others. Positive people seem to accept death with grace.

I have faced the possibility of death - even though remotely - only twice. As I told you, once in an airplane when the landing gear wouldn't come down and we circled forever getting rid of fuel. The runway was foamed and I held you, a mere baby, in my arms as tightly as I could. People were crying. Just as we were making an emergency landing the wheels came down and we cheered and then, I cried for joy!

The second time, as you know, was 9/11 when we didn't know if it was the end. Neither time was I brave. Both times I was scared and worried I would never see you again.

But, we were "together" both times and for that I feel so fortunate.

Dear daughter, have you ever faced your own death? The way we live is often the way we die.

"The Helping Verbs"

Believing that the helping verbs never got enough attention, I memorized them in third grade and use them from time to time, mostly to put me to sleep:

is
be
am
are
was
were
been
do
does
did
has
have
had
may
might
shall
should
will
would

Try saying them as fast as you can.

For a while I called Max "is be" which became "IZBY." And later I named him "been do" which became "BINDO." Helping verbs for a helpful guy! How crazy is this?

April 27, 2003

"Silence on a Sunday"

Today is my day of silence. I am doing it for the following reasons:

1. To explore the power of silence.
2. To allow me to meditate and to think without distraction.
3. To change the structure of the day.
4. To make good on a pact with Donna.

All good reasons. Report? No big revelations; just felt closer to cat Esme who rarely "speaks."

Monette: I urge you to try this.

"It's Up to You"
   Today is a day the Lord has made.
   Make it a good one.

April 29, 2003

"Onomatopoeia"

This time of year brings the grumbles. It's a bit too early for flowers, bathing suits, and vacations so workers tend to grumble more. In higher education it also is nearing the end of the spring term. There are year-end reports to create, reviews to write and lots of events to plan. Thus the workload on staff is at a peak and we all have a case for the grumbles.

Grumble is one of those great words that sounds like its meaning. Thus, an onomatopoeia. Did you study these? Here are some that come to mind:

salubrious
flesh
whisk
whistle
runaround
delicious
flabbergasted
glorious
hallowed
whipped cream
antiquated
bulbous
cunning
devious
empty
fragrance
gigantic
rambunctious
brilliant
loquacious
hubris

DIANE FAY SKOMARS

It isn't only that we attach meaning to the word. It is that when we *say these words out loud*, they sound like their definition. Use onomatopoeias! You get double the impact.

"What Does It Take to Have a Hit Show?"

Tonight Max and I saw a play. You had warned me about the poor script. I am ashamed to admit it, but we actually left at intermission. I had been up since 5 a.m. and kept falling asleep.

What makes a great production? I have seen excellent scripts plus excellent acting and directing with great lights and set, a full house, and yet, the production is mediocre. And I have witnessed the opposite - ordinary script, actors, and set, and MAGIC happens. You are in a crazy business. Agreed?

I know you believe that the audience plays a large part in the success of any production. I understand that concept, but I must say that without a strong performance, the audience does not a hit make.

May I get your thinking on this matter again, please?

May 1, 2003

WHITE RABBIT! You got me!

****

"From Trash to Art"

Maxi said the funniest thing to me last evening. As we watched yet another dumb commercial on television he said, "When we see such a commercial as this one, we call it trash, but when one of our kids is in it, it becomes art!"

"Misunderstanding"

Tonight Max and I had a misunderstanding! I hate them but it sure can happen.

I was at an alumni event in the Twin Cities and was to meet Max at 8:30 p.m. at our hotel. He had left me a message that he would be an hour late.

So at 9:30 I went to the lobby to wait for him hoping we could have a drink and start the weekend together. After an hour, I began to worry about a car accident.

He showed up at 11:00 p.m. No call. (No cell phones.) He got stuck with his friends who got lost. I sure felt let down and mad. We fussed and finally made up later. Hate those misunderstandings. My biggest enemy at these times is always fatigue.

Once I stated my keen disappointment and admitted how tired I was, I could let go of my frustration. I also listened to his words, "I am sorry."

How do you handle such misunderstandings?

"*A Mighty Wind*"

I saw this film today. When Nana and Pops began taking me to the movies, I learned the delicious nature of the complete escape and the utter seduction of a great story. I was hooked. To this day I still love to go to a movie and get into the film-zone. What is it about that darkened cave, faded draperies, the crunch of popcorn and bigger-than-life gangsters, heroes, and beautiful people moving before you? Earliest memorable movies include *The Thing*, *The House of Wax*, and *The Long, Long Trailer*.

As I wrote earlier, when you were a toddler you loved seeing *New York, New York*. I took you to all the films I went to and you were good as gold in the last row where you ate animal crackers, enjoyed "spider juice" (instead of "cider juice"), and whispered sweet revelations in my ear. We called movies our "whispering times."

What are your favorite films of all times?

May 4, 2003

"Retirement"

    I attended a retirement party today. It will be difficult for me to make the decision about when to retire. I am not clear yet about how to stay active and healthy and sane once I let go of a title, salary, and job.

    A friend told me that no matter what you are told, you do not have enough money and the phone does not ring. In other words, it is a time for redefinition of self, or re-invention. I can imagine staying busy but I cannot imagine it adding up to much. We all need to feel needed.

    Other advice I have been given: 1. You can only quit once. Don't ever say, "I am thinking about retiring in two years" or they will be creating a search committee before you get back to your office. 2. Never let others plan your retirement party. It is yours to own and pay for, if you are able. 3. Volunteer for something right away. 4. Don't volunteer because it seems like work. 5. Create your own agenda based on passion and long neglected interests. 6. When you miss having a title, say to yourself every morning, "I am a very important person!" 7. Travel, travel, travel. 8. Learn something new every day. 9. Help someone else every day.

    I believe I will know when I am finished because I will have given my all to my university and will sense that "new blood" will bring renewed commitment to the institution. I also know that I will be bone weary of meetings, work travel, and being tied to a computer. As you know, I HATE COMPUTERS! So someday I will retire and it will be different... but eventually good by me.

    Are you too young to even contemplate retirement?

DIANE FAY SKOMARS

May 5, 2003

"Monette Fay and Diane Fay in the Big Apple"

"Lay Off"

We had to "lay off" a valued staff person. It was so difficult because I am very fond of this person. But budget cuts are just that.

Patty was amazing because when Bill and I told her, she stayed in the moment and told us how she felt and what she was thinking and then said, "Perhaps something better is out there for me." She will no doubt go through anger, disbelief, distancing and finally resolution, and it will be very difficult. Because she is so very talented, she will land on her feet no doubt doing "something better."

No one was happy with this decision, and I lay awake most of the night hating my role in it.

Although our connection at the university will be over, I hope we can stay in touch and work on other projects. Lesson: Always leave the door open when you value someone.

"Bob, May He Rest in Peace"

Bob died today. We go back a long way with this good family. I once worked for Hommey and Bruce. Claudia once worked with me. Claudia refinished the lovely antique rocker for you when you were born. Hommey and I are in a women's group together. Claudia and I share our mutual (one day apart) birthdays together. Bob opened the door for your first movie part in Hollywood. Bob and Hommey gave Max and me a party at their home when we were first married.

There are friends and there are friends, but there is nothing like old friends.

Our lives have been enriched by these good people.

Which friends have been there for *you* over many years?

May 8, 2003

"Mountain Gorillas"

Did you ever wonder why I have a framed photograph of a mountain gorilla among our pictures of family members?

Thanks to my friend Patsy who inspired it and friend Deb who enhanced it mightily, our trip to Rwanda to visit these gorillas was a mountain top experience. The photograph reminds me that we are "brothers and sisters of all living things."

We trekked for miles on end to find these beautiful creatures. We were taught how to act when we met them: head down, no eye contact, munch on bamboo shoots. They were peaceful but curious about us and we were respectful. It was a very emotional experience for me, and I cried. As we slowly backed out of the area, one member of our team, Paul, said to me, "Well, that's the first mountain gorilla that ever met me!" Cracked me up.

Later that night, while we slept in a tin hut trying to identify exotic animal noises all around us, friend Eleanor and I talked and laughed until we hit dreamland.

Let's go together on a photographic safari, Mosie.

"Do Justly, Love Mercy, Walk Humbly With Thy God" (Micah 6:8)

Bob was buried today. The service was very special. Rabbi Amy spoke eloquently about Bob and wept herself during the service. Bob's philosophy was: "Do justly, love mercy, walk humbly with thy God."

The burial was in wet, cold and windy weather. We each added a shovel of dirt until the casket was covered. The Rabbi spoke about life and death (and weather) being "messy." By adding a shovel of dirt, Bob's leaving seemed more real to me and his life more vivid. A very memorable service.

Never avoid funerals, Monette. They help the "loved ones" cope with the death, and they help the dead transfer to the other side knowing their life was not in vain.

May 10, 2003

"A Grand Escape"

How I love the road! I left work at 4:30 p.m. and drove half way to Chicago to surprise the Max tomorrow night at his performance! It was raining, cold and windy but I was in my cocoon of a car, safe and happy and listening to books-on-tape and Max Morath CD's.

Do you love the road? Where do you want to travel by car?

"Mother's Day"

Thank you for always making me feel like a million on "Mother's Day." Your cards and sentiments and calls and gifts (opened early) are wonderful! You are such a loving daughter.

On Mother's Day I imagine lining up with all the women in direct lineage...you, me, Nana, Grandma Johnson, Great Grandma Niemi, and on and on. I literally see us standing tall, not touching of course (we're Finns), full of strength and courage, looking to the future. You, my dear daughter, are our future. Create a good one for yourself and others. We are all behind you.

I love you with all my heart.

May 12, 2003

"Nebber Gibbup, Nebber Gibbin."

You and I spoke tonight about your possibilities: Arena Stage, La Jolla Playhouse, Pasadena Playhouse. What a sweet time in your life to consider your possible future onstage at these fine theatres.

Never give up, never give in...or as Max says, "Nebber gibbup, nebber gibbin."

"Flying Up"

Today I gave a young friend a purse I purchased in Chicago that features a woman looking in the mirror. I wrote: "Always like who you see when looking in a mirror."

This idea of a woman looking into a mirror and really seeing herself came to me from Brownies, the first step of Girl Scouts. When a girl "flies up" to Girl Scouts, she is asked to look in a mirror and to behold herself just as she is...at least that is how we used to do it. I always liked that idea - not to gaze upon the self to better the vision for others, but to look deep into your eyes and to own yourself and to like yourself "just as you are."

Do you like yourself, Mosie?

May 14, 2003

"Tending Our Garden"

The media conference announcing a generous gift of 4.5 million went off without a hitch. It begins the funding for a new, much needed building for the Labovitz School of Business and Economics at UMD. It is the dream of many people. A gift of this size has star players: the donor couple and their family members, the Chancellor, the Dean, the faculty and staff and students, the university itself, the legislature. And this new building follows two other stellar buildings, the Weber Music Hall and the Swenson Science Building, all given by alumni of UMD.

It was a joyous occasion on our campus, but what I will remember of the day was the donor's comment, "My wife and I look at this gift as *tending our garden.*" This inspired statement set the tone for the day and the gift. Notice, his statement wasn't about the money; it was about the sentiment behind it. That is what I love about development. It brings out the very best in good people.

Ask yourself each day, "What am I giving to others today and why am I doing it?"

"Matchmaking"

I have tried three times to be a matchmaker. Each time the parties called after their dates and said, in effect, "You've got to be kidding!" Clearly not my calling.

Have you ever tried to match-make? How did it turnout?

"You Asked Me for a List of Some of My Favorite Films"

1. *Babette's Feast*
2. *Planes, Trains and Automobiles*
3. *To Kill a Mockingbird*
4. *Love Actually*
5. *Much Ado About Nothing*
6. *A Place in the Sun*
7. *The Legend of 1900*
8. *Enchanted April*
9. *Who's Afraid of Virginia Woolf?*
10. *North by Northwest*
11. *African Queen*
12. *Fried Green Tomatoes*
13. *Atlantic City*
14. *Witness for the Prosecution*
15. *Scenes from a Marriage*
16. *Cape Fear*
17. *Guess Who's Coming for Dinner*
18. *Fargo*
19. *Best in Show*
20. *Silence of the Lambs*

"Commencement"

930 UMD students "commenced" today with 5,000 attendees. My friend Lucy directed this entire successful event. Do you remember your NYU commencement and further back, your high school graduation? I sat with your grandparents to watch you graduate from Hickman High School, and four years later with Max in NY. He had received an M.A. from Columbia University the day before you got your NYU diploma. A heady time for my family.

I love commencements and I dream of giving the following speech: "Graduates, this is your day. GIVE IN to your feelings of separation from that which you have known, and the fear of the future. GIVE UP the notion that you did it alone. You have many to thank. GIVE BACK to those who helped you and to the university that inspired you." But no one has ever asked me.

What would you tell the graduates?

May 18, 2003

"Rock in My Shoe"

Today was supposed to be a day without cares. A day of leisure and peace.

However, it was the day I heard from someone to whom I had written about an issue that was bugging me. We clearly disagree about it and things were said I regret. I hate confrontation and disagreements. The price is too high. Even if this clears the air, things will never be the same.

I should have torn up the note and never sent it. Today would have been a lot better that way. But am not sure future days would have been any good since I would have still been stewing about it.

There is a price to clearing the air. And there is a price to carrying a rock in your shoe.

"Rain, Rain, Go Away. Come Again Some Other Day"

It is all about rain today...a steady rainfall from sunrise to sunset. It is a comfort in a way because it softens the day and takes the edge off most folks. It certainly works that way for me.

Of course the basement is flooded in our cottage and puddles form the path to the garage and back, and the house feels damp even with the heater on.

Cat Esme is outside but hugging the house under the eaves to protect herself as she makes her way in.

How does the weather affect you, my born-in-Minnesota daughter?

"Damiana"

A special gift arrived today from my friend Patsy. I received a bottle of "Damiana" - a rum drink from Mexico. It is the same bottle she brought back from our trip to Baja to study whales, to remind me of our escapade.

On our vacation in Mexico, Patsy was determined to find a liquor store, buy the rum, and bring it home. (The bottle is distinct and in the form of a shapely woman.) We had just come off a whale watch onboard a small vessel for a week, and were spending a bit of time relaxing at a hotel. Patsy set off to find Damiana, and I told her she needed company so off we went. Our Spanish was less than limited so we got nowhere in the first store. Then a guy came along and offered to drive us to a store that featured the drink, at least that is what we thought he said in Spanish. Ever trusting Patsy said, "Great." We got into his car and he drove to the police station! We thought we were really in trouble until his wife, a police officer, came out and got into the car. Next we drove to a childcare center to pick up their boys. We were all trying to communicate but with no luck.

Next all six of us went to their home where they locked the doors and entertained us with music by the Beatles and offered strong liqueurs. They serenaded us with song and began dancing. It got stranger, and we asked to leave but they offered more drink and singing. We began to get worried because we had been gone many hours and no one else in our group knew where we were. Neither did we. It felt like we were being kidnapped. Finally, after we pleaded our case to leave, our host brought us back to where we started. (Looking back, they were probably just trying to be friendly.) Our friends thought we had been abducted and were about to go to the police.

Patsy, of course, still wanted her Damiana! Later we found it and today I got that very same bottle in the mail in honor of my upcoming 60th birthday. I laughed until I cried remembering this trip and the others, one to Rwanda to visit the mountain gorillas and the other to the Solomon Islands. I thank Patsy every day for her spirit and generosity. A real friend. Advice: Save your life stories as if they were pearls on a string to wear and remember.

May 21, 2003

"Inverting the Introvert"

We introverts ought to unite and form an organization that explains us to the rest of the universe. As a person who scores off the charts as an "Introvert" on the personality inventory tests, I think I can start the list. Here is what I believe:

1. We do not have to talk all the time. We shy away from those who do.
2. We cross the street to avoid eye contact.
3. It is better that we live in NYC rather than in the woods, where we feel trapped by anyone who approaches us. NYC offers anonymity.
4. While at the cinema, we sit as far away from others as possible. We often don't select a seat until everyone else is seated.
5. If we are forced to attend a reception in a room full of strangers, we will be invisible until we find the other introvert in the room and we head straight toward him/her. Introverts can always find each other. We often find other introverts to be the most interesting of all those gathered, because they haven't given it away by telling all to everyone.
6. We may be good conversationalists on the job, but tongue-tied at an intimate dinner party of new people.
7. We hate B & B's - too close and personal.
8. We love talking one-to-one.
9. Our social contact glass fills up twice as fast as the extrovert's.
10. Only our loved ones understand our withdrawals into ourselves when we are exhausted from too much talk.

DIANE FAY SKOMARS

"Inverting the Introvert" continued...

11. We are often in the arts and hide behind the written word, the paintbrush, the song, or the character we portray.
12. We operate well in "spill-over spotlight" but not comfortably in the spotlight.
13. We are great observers of others.
14. We can praise others but not receive praise from them.
15. We usually think before we speak.
16. When I get home from work, Max often asks me, "Tell me about your day." I always respond, "Not yet. Can't talk. Give me an hour."

What are your results on personality inventory tests? Are you an introvert?

By the way, I just heard from friend Jeanne about the book, *The Introvert Advantage: How to Thrive in an Extrovert World* by Marti Olsen Laney.

May 23, 2003

"Quebec City"

We are visiting Quebec for our anniversary (and my birthday) and loving it! Because it has the flavor of France and the robust atmosphere of Canada, I feel right at home. And it is a city of romance.

Some of the most exotic cities I have visited are: Hanoi, Rovaniemi, Istanbul, Cape Town, Puerto Vallarta, St. Petersburg, New York, Todi, Marrakech, Dharamshala, Guadalcanal, and Saint-Pierre et Miquelon.

Each has an element of excitement, intrigue and a dash of romance. And the food is good! Perhaps it is what happened to me in each of these places that bring them to mind. Better yet, what could happen if I were to return.

At any rate we are enjoying this beautiful city while holding hands, dining out, and speaking French to each other (ha!). How fortunate we are to have found each other in this world of mismatches.

May 24, 2003

"Happy 60th Birthday to Moi!"

A good day with a lovely meal at L'Amour Restaurant here in Quebec City. Lobster! Layered chocolate mousse cake. Fine French wine and a classic Caesar prepared tableside. If I am ever on death row, this will be the last meal I will request.

Maxie treated me special all day and he bought me a necklace made by "Lunch at the Ritz." How can I be so fortunate?

I know I am expected to act differently now that I am 60 years of age, but I think I will pass on that idea and instead plow ahead at full speed.

Thanks for your gift and messages. They mean a lot!

"Summer Vegetable Soup" (Thanks to Beatrice A. Ojakangas and her *Finnish Cookbook.*)

15 tiny new (or 2 or 3 larger) carrots
1 cup sweet new peas
2 cups tiny snap beans (or larger beans cut into 2-inch pieces)
3 sweet new onions, chopped
2 cups tiniest new potatoes (for larger potatoes, cubed)
1 tablespoon sugar
1 teaspoon salt
2 tablespoons flour
4 cups whole milk (or for an elegant version,1/2 and 1/2 cream)
2 tablespoons butter
chopped parsley

Clean the carrots (cut large carrots into 2-inch sticks and quarter them lengthwise). Scrub the new potatoes to remove the thin peel, but peel the larger ones. Put the carrots, peas, beans, onions, and potatoes into a pot. Add boiling water just to cover. Cook for 5 minutes or until the vegetables are almost tender. In another pot, combine the sugar, salt, flour, and milk and bring to a boil. Pour into the pot of vegetables and simmer for 10 minutes. Pour into a soup tureen, dot with butter, and garnish with the parsley. Serve hot. Serves 4 to 6.

I love Bea's soup, and I envy the fact that you have access to your Farmer's Market year around. Take advantage!

"No Fear of Flying"

Did I ever tell you I levitated as a child right in our living room? I don't believe I ever told anyone except my NY shrink. I don't think you will believe me, but it is true.

It was a wonderful escape. It was always the same. I was alone in the living room with the sun pouring in and with a gentle jump, up I would go until I was horizontal to the ceiling. I could navigate the room and I felt euphoric. I also remember exactly how I came down to the carpet.

The only other times I have felt that good were under water scuba diving, ice skating alone on a frozen river, running while training for the marathon, and sitting on a deck chair crossing the Atlantic.

Where does euphoria come from? For me it comes from a bit of adventure or sitting among strangers on the high seas.

Where and when do you feel such delicious escape?

May 27, 2003

"My Ever-Changing Lake Superior"

     The lake is as still as glass. The birds skim over the water in perfect formation. An ore boat, far out to sea, cuts through the calm surface and creates a deep path that folds into itself.

     Two weeks ago we still had ice in the harbor. Now it is 75 degrees with bugs, birds, and all that is spring. It happens overnight here. Winter, yesterday and today spring.

"My Music Man"

Max played a private concert for me tonight. His lovely melodies transformed me into a more loving and compassionate person. Does music affect you in that way?

May 29, 2003

"Call Back"

Today they called you back for a second audition. And today you thanked me for listening to you last night when you felt distraught over your career.

You said I was "safe" to talk to. I sure appreciated your telling me that. Thank you!

Do you believe your ups and downs in the theatrical business will ever change?

"Birthday Bliss"

We drove to Gilbert and had dinner at the "Whistling Bird," a Jamaican restaurant in Northern Minnesota. Pat and brother Buzz treated us for my birthday and our anniversary. It was so good to be with my family!

This got me thinking about past birthdays. Nana always gathered my girlfriends for my May 24th celebration. As little girls, we wore full-skirted party dresses with patent-leather shoes and paper hats. Our hair was in ringlets and our socks featured lace! We played "Pin the Tail on the Donkey" and "Drop the Clothes Pin in the Bottle." There were prizes for winners and gifts for me: a book, hankie, pin, or days-of-the-week underwear. The best was the dark chocolate layer cake Nana made and the favors for each of us. I also remember little paper cups filled with mint candies and peanuts. "Remember to thank everyone," said Nana.

One year it snowed in Duluth on May 24th so the out-of-doors birthday photograph was cancelled!

My brothers were never invited to my birthday parties nor were they interested. This year, however, it was lovely to blow out my candles with Pat, Max and one of my brothers present at the table. (My wish was for a role for you.)

Lesson for the day: Always celebrate your own birthday the way you want and with whom you want. June 2nd is your very own day, Monette.

May 31, 2003

"Isolation"
       If you separate yourself from others by:
       gender
       age
       race
       attractiveness
       politics
       intelligence
       and wealth,
       you will end up alone.

June 1, 2003

WHITE RABBIT!!! Got you!

************************** *****************************

"Star to Come"

> "Twinkle, twinkle, little star,
> How I wonder what you are!
> Up above the world so high,
> Like a diamond in the sky.
> Twinkle, twinkle, little star,
> How I wonder what you are!"
>
> Poem by Jane Taylor from *The Golden Book of Poetry, 1947*
> Your very first poem, my dear. There are actually four more

verses, but this was your favorite. Have you ever written a poem?

> If not, try it, right now.

June 2, 2003

"Twenty-nine Candles"

Happy, Happy Birthday, Mosie.
Twenty-nine and divine!
Hope you like the earrings.

You were almost born on the beach of the St. Croix River in Stillwater, Minnesota. We had taken our dear friends, the Siggel-kows, out on our houseboat, the *Hello Dolly*. My water broke as I sat on a sandy beach but I didn't tell anyone, not wanting to spoil their fun. I was wearing a large muumuu and sat upon a beach towel. Our friends left the river at dusk and I told your Father we had better go home and pack. We left for the hospital about 10:30 p.m. because I was determined to not get there too early. The nurse in charge said, "Since this is your first child, wait until midnight and you won't be charged for an extra day." So we checked in at 12 and you were born around 3 a.m.! By the way, while I was moaning and groaning, the nurse didn't believe I was in serious labor because, "This is your first baby." She seemed embarrassed and surprised when you came so quickly.

I was hoping to be knocked out, but you came fast and there was no time. A child, who had been in a car accident, was being helped by my doctor. I remember praying for that child and for you. I also remember singing "Help Me Make it Through the Night." Upon your arrival, the nurse said, "She's perfect." And you were. I told you, "If I had known it was you, Baby Girl, I'd have had you sooner."

"A Bit of Sparkle"

You said you like the tiny diamond earrings. Hoorah! Some of my girlfriends thought I should have waited until you turned 30 but I don't believe in postponing expressions of love.

I hope you wear them for auditions, wear them to the gym, wear them scrubbing floors, and wear them to an opening.

Once I had lovely diamond earrings from Max, and I wore them on a trip to NY. I forgot to pack the box they came in, so I wrapped those lovely gems in Kleenex (!) and carefully tucked them deep in my purse. (You *know* where this story is going.) Two days later, I cleaned out my purse and threw out all the Kleenex!!! I couldn't bring myself to tell Max or you. My only hope was that a hotel maid found the sparkling earrings and still wears them.

Advice: when you travel, keep your diamonds on you at all times or leave them at home in the box they came in and hide it the Cheerios box.

June 4, 2003

"You, Through a Mother's Eyes"

Whenever I asked Nana what I was like as a child, she answered in terms of achievements (little awards, music, grades, photographs, performances). I swore I would never do that to you. So here are some of my remembrances of you as a small child.

You were a clown, a very funny little girl. Always entertaining real or imaginary guests, dressing up for every occasion, creating whole scenes using your dolls and stuffed animals and my clothes and jewelry.

You always had one best friend and were devoted to this person and were exceptionally loyal.

At age six, your first 'boyfriend" came to play at Eastcliff for a few hours on a Saturday. Upon arriving at the door, his mother announced, "He bathed with Irish Spring this morning." You said, "That's okay, we can still play."

Your room was well organized and you never destroyed a book. You lined up your books, and your dolls and stuffed toys according to your devotion to them.

You loved to draw and paint. I have a photograph of you in Finland when you were two, painting up a storm with your beautiful cousin, Mia. Your designs were bold and free.

You had a strong sense of right and wrong and knew when you made a mistake. In the third grade, you wrote a note to your best friend describing the substitute teacher but using "bad words." The note was intercepted and you were sent to the head master. Your punishment was to write a paragraph giving the details, and bring it home and have your parents sign it. The last sentence was, "I have learned not to put my feelings in writing." It was difficult for me not to laugh over the last sentence! But I couldn't because you were crying and really upset. Because you were so hard on yourself, there was no need to add more punishment.

DIANE FAY SKOMARS

"You, Through a Mother's Eyes" continued...

You loved to shop. At one point when you were in junior high, you asked for a meeting with me and sat me down and said, "Look, I know you don't like to change things, but we need a microwave for quick meals and after school snacks, and you need to buy it today. Now, get dressed and let's go to the mall." And we did.

You were smart, just plain smart. Smart in school. Smart about expressing yourself and smart about knowing who you were and what you liked and didn't like. You came into this world with a clear sense of self and I have always admired that in you.

You are a softy about animals and all living creatures. We always had cats and dogs and, in Missouri, a horse. Your voice changed when talking to the pets. It was like you shared a special communion with them.

Although my earliest memory of you is of you smiling in the morning when I entered your room and peeked in your crib, you are not a morning person.

You loved to be read to and eventually to read yourself. You always had your nose in a book and loved the same stories over and over. On one occasion when I changed the ending of Cinderella to, "Cinderella went on to become a lawyer and the Prince stayed home with their children," you were furious. "That's not what it says, Momma!"

When you were in junior high, I was reading a personal ad from a woman who said she was seeking a SWM (single, white, male). I said, "Why on earth would a woman limit herself to white men?" And you said, "Good grief! That is her preference. Not everything is about civil rights, Mother!"

June 6, 2003

"You, Through a Mother's Eyes" continued...

When we lived in Eastcliff and entertained 4,000 people per year in this University President's Residence, I gave tours of the entire house, not just the downstairs. I believed it was a public home and all of it belonged to the people of the state. It meant our quarters had to be "visitor ready."

After yet another group had walked through your bedroom and greeted you, you asked me, "Why are all these people coming to see *me*?" You were but four years of age.

You saw through people and did not suffer fools. You knew who was kind, and trustworthy and who was not.

And you were dramatic. Nana called you "a summer storm... soon over but memorable." Yes, you were high and low and full of drama. A burst of energy as you entered any room. You were a born leader and others listened to you, including your mother. It wasn't a matter of giving in to you, but rather, often liking your idea or solution better than my own.

What are your strongest memories of growing up?

DIANE FAY SKOMARS

"Three Weddings and No Funeral"

Richard gave me you, and we were "kids" of our times.

Peter showed me the world and helped raise you.

Maxie offered joy and laughter.

Remembering only the good times, I loved them all. All three are smart. All three are Episcopalians. Not one dances.

"Hubert H. Humphrey"

When I was a little girl, I often spent a week each summer with my grandparents on their farm in Cedar Valley. It made a strong impression on me. They were exceptional people to be with, and it was loads of fun to visit my lively cousins (especially Debbie, Gloria, Mona and Lisa) at the farms of Nana's brothers Leo (and Elina, the well-known columnist, who sends us special handmade cards) and Bruno (and Fran). I was always made to feel welcome.

My earliest memory of my grandparents' log home with a wood-burning stove, was listening to Finnish music on their radio. I remember they had two pictures, one of Minnesota's Hubert Humphrey and one of Jesus Christ. I figured out that they both must be very important men.

You know about the life of Jesus Christ, of course. But do you know about Hubert Humphrey? He was the Vice President under President Lyndon Johnson, and he also ran for President of the United States in 1968. Vice President Humphrey lost the presidency to Richard Nixon. I believe he lost because of his loyalty to President Johnson, who was mired in the blood of the Viet Nam War.

Hubert Horatio Humphrey was a humanitarian, a smart Minnesota politician, and kind of unsung hero. In 1948 he gave one of the most powerful speeches on civil rights ever given. I met him several times and he looked me straight in the eye and said, "How are you, Diane?" No, never mind that I was wearing a nametag.

Years ago we attended an event honoring Hubert Humphrey near the end of his life at the Vice President's Residence when the Mondales lived there. It was a heady occasion for both Peter and me when we met everyone from Liz Taylor to Henry Kissinger. Besides the graciousness of the Mondales, I recall feeling very fortunate to sit next to Lorne Greene who was a class act and asked me about *my* life in Minnesota. Can you imagine that? Who are your political heroes, Miss Monette?

"Elaine Stritch"

Three hours alone on stage in Minneapolis. Her show was first rate.

I expected the candor, comedy, and outrageous attitude. What I didn't expect was the excellent script, pace and depth, and the emotion. Had tears at the end. What courage it takes to turn the spotlight on your own life. It is one thing to act a role of someone else's creation, but quite another to act out your very own past. She did it well and she made me think about the power of storytelling.

The act of writing down what I believe to be true, for you, is another kind of leap of faith. I know the minute I am done with this year of lessons and advice, I will think of all that I have forgotten to tell you.

Can you imagine creating a one-woman show about your life? What would it include?

"Yoga"

This morning I participated in an hour of yoga. It was a great way to begin the day. There are 20 in my class. I hope to make it twice a week. It feels so good to stretch and to take time to do something for myself.

Except for playing first base on a girls' team, I never was an exercise person or a jock, nor did I ever pay much attention to the workings of my body. But when we lived in NY, I worked out with a trainer at a 24-hour, tough gym in lower Manhattan. The first time I visited was pretty intimidating. I was the only person over 55 years of age, female, and without muscle. The sweat, testosterone, mingled with youth and rippling muscle were heady stuff and I loved the company. My patient trainer brought me through my paces and I really enjoyed those hours trying to build up strength, fluidity of movement, and coordination. And the men began to greet me as a regular. Very cool.

Do you remember when I brought you there to meet my trainer? The lesson for today is to take care of your body. It is the only one you've got! And the more you move, the more you move.

"Elias, Elmer, Isaac"

On June 15, 1920, three African American men were beaten, tortured and hung in Duluth, falsely accused of raping a white woman. Although they are referred to as CLAYTON-JACKSON-McGHIE, I like to remember them as Elias Clayton, Elmer Jackson, Isaac McGhie. No one should die surrounded by hate, surrounded by strangers. No one should be put to death accused of a crime and have no access to a defense.

Today I drove to their gravesite and left flowers. They are close to Nana and Pop's grave, so I can stop by from time to time.

We, as a community, cannot change the past, but we can face the fact after years of silence. Duluth citizens now have a weeklong commemoration and a teach-in about race relations. In addition, donations have been collected to create life-size bronze statues. There is hope, too late for some, but not too late for others. History teaches us lessons of life if only we would remember and learn.

"New York, New York"

I saw the Broadway play, *Enchanted April*, today with Donna. Getting tickets at the last minute, Hommey and Claudia were there also. We all loved it.

Because the movie remains one of my favorites, I worried the theatrical treatment would never measure up, but it did!

I am reminded that there are so many wonderful advantages to the stage. As a movie maven, this is hard to admit. The nuances between actors, the "alive" quality, and the potential danger involved in real time drama make for an exciting adventure.

I guess, good is good, no matter what the form.

June 13, 2003

"Trust Everyone...But Cut the Cards"

It takes guts to write a musical adapted from the writings of Finley Peter Dunne, and put it on stage in NYC. Max did it and it was wonderful! Loved the music. Bravo, Maxie!

Max Morath is so much more than an entertainer, composer, writer. He is a whole person, smart and witty, charming and kind, and very funny. I swear I married him for his humor above all else. I love that in him.

I had dinner with Kathy and Christy. I thought about how beautiful they are and how Max's three children each have special qualities of his. Kathy has his theatrical and musical talent and drive; Christy has his quest for learning and his keen intelligence; and Fred has his kindness and sweet nature. Obviously, each has all these qualities, but I was struck by their strong individual connections to their Daddy.

I also got to thinking about what you and I share besides the fact that we are both Geminis. It sometimes feels like we are of one mind and other times our thinking is worlds apart, as it should be. The mother/daughter connection is very tricky business, Monette, and I used to worry that we are too close. When I asked my shrink about it, she responded "Don't be ridiculous, Diane. Be glad you are on speaking terms."

My dad was always a hero, but it is Nana that I write mostly about in these pages for you. She was the one who set the bar for me, taught me what she knew, and modeled female behavior. We are, of course, a composite of all the primary influences in our lives.

I know what Max's children inherited from him and their mother, but I ask you, what did you receive from each parent?

"Channeling"

Today is "Father's Day" and I am remembering Pops.

Did I ever tell you about Pops "visiting" me after his death? The first time, I was at a session on "channeling" that my friend's daughter was leading. I had never done anything like this before, but I wanted to support this young woman. She did a series of exercises including "sending" imagined colored balls around the circle as she asked us to identify the color of each ball. I clearly "saw" the color of the balls. She had my attention.

After a few other exercises, we were asked to go into a kind of trance and to ask our guide to introduce us to the "higher guide" and to repeat the request with the next guide. Eventually I "saw" a golden door with light behind it. When I "climbed" the steps leading to the door, I again asked for my "higher guide." The door opened and there was radiant light. I asked, "Who are you?" And the answer came back, "E.T, of course," in Pop's voice. ("E.T." was Pop's initials, you will recall, and he was often called that.) Tears ran down my cheeks and I was laughing because it was so comforting and funny.

The second time was in St. Louis on a hotel's patio while having brunch with Max. We had just begun dating and Pop's vague image bathed in bright light stood behind Max. "He is a good man," Pop's said, and then he was gone. Max asked me at whom I was staring. "My dad came to visit," was my reply. Max never asked anything more.

The third time was at a vineyard in Missouri and again I was with Max. Pops again stood behind Max, said nothing, and just departed. I have never "seen" Pops since.

I like to think that Pops was just making sure I was okay. I cry as I write this because it is so vivid and I miss him. I know for sure that he will help me "go over" when my time comes. And Nana will be making my room "visitor ready."

June 15, 2003

"Richard"

Your father, Richard, has his birthday in June. Although we represented different schools, we both participated in high school speech competitions. We didn't connect again until UMD where we ended up active in student government and other student organizations.

In the sixties, politics mattered and we were committed to the anti-war movement. Before you were born, we participated in the 1971 Peace March on Washington. By most accounts, it was the largest peace rally to date. As Richard reminds me, John Kerry, representing the Viet Nam Veterans Against the War, spoke from the steps of the capitol. This peace march remains one of the most memorable events in my life.

Our generation knew the Viet Nam War was wrong and we argued with family and friends, and even in Duluth marched against it. That war defined a lot of us and still haunts the nation. We not only lost the war, some took it out on our soldiers. A horrible time.

Richard came from a military family and because of their moving, he attended 13 schools growing up. In just one year alone, he was in three different schools. Given his background, it had to be more difficult for Richard to speak up against the Viet Nam War than it was for me.

It seems unusual now to write about a marriage in terms of a peace movement, but I am recalling the strength of our conviction and how our shared values gave us a very special bond.

You, however, were our best effort.

"President George W. Bush"

The one-day trip to the White House with our UMD Championship Women's Hockey Team went well.

The President was most gracious. Last year the President urged our students to participate in a volunteer program of some kind. This year they told him they were "Big Sisters" to kids; volunteered at the Humane Society; and were committed to tutoring children. He listened and was pleased and he publicly recognized our Chancellor Martin. Am so proud of our Bulldog women! (By the way, I met a new friend, Mimmu, from Finland who works for our Coach Shannon.)

Although I am not a Republican, and I have been known to rail against the policies of the Bush administration, I must say I saw President Bush in a new light. As he stood before us honoring the students as leader athletes, the President was most generous. As my brother Buzz says, "Always give someone his due."

Advice: never think of people as all good or all bad. Each of us possesses qualities of both.

June 17, 2003

"Senator Hillary Rodham Clinton"

When I saw the Senator at the White House event, I knew I would meet her. So in spite of the hordes of people surrounding her, I thrust out my hand and said,

"Senator, you are a hero. I just read your autobiography and it inspired me."

"God bless you," she said.

DIANE FAY SKOMARS

"Hillary Rodham Clinton" by Lucy Kragness

June 19, 2003

"Get Back on the Horse"

You've had some disappointing auditions. It seems you have to have about seven to twelve auditions before a "hit."

I admire the way you "get back on the horse."

Did you ever think your beloved horse, "Trustee," would teach you so much?

June 20, 2003

"Worth the Trust" ("Trustee")

"Fish Story"

Fishing goes back in our family for as long as I can remember. Years ago I corresponded with a sea captain named Skomars from Turku, Finland. Pop's family fished Lake Superior from a wooden boat. I can remember as a little girl, Nana saying, "Reel it in. The wind has changed. Here comes a storm." And with Pop's 25 horsepower motor at full throttle, we would head for shore as fast as we could.

Nana's father fished the local rivers and lakes in Northern Minnesota and featured the fish in Grandma's mojakka. This hearty dish was tasty but it sometimes required viewing the head of the dead fish. Harsh.

But the real test of loving fish was dining on lutefisk during the holidays. Cod soaked first in lye does not an appetite make. The putrid smell in the house during the cooking process brings about unintentional fighting, the flight of domestic pets, and tears to the eyes of otherwise stalwart men. When Maxie and I married, I insisted he do two things...go into Lake Superior over his head and eat a plate of lutefisk. He survived both, barely.

Next Christmas I plan to make you lutefisk. Something for you to look forward to, my dear. It is important to keep family traditions going!

"More on Fishing"

Nana and Pops owned a fishing boat, the *MONTOY*, and we fished and camped most weekends of the summer. (I missed summer dances because we were fishing!) What do I remember?

The scavenging/howling sounds of wildlife at night: fox, bear, raccoons, rabbits, squirrels, wolves.

The bright sun of summer and sunbathing in the boat and hoping no fish would hit my line or I would have to move.

The time Pops challenged me to waterski around an entire lake and I did!

The times my friend Janet and her family joined us, and she and I would lie in the tent talking about boys, and reading *Seventeen* magazine. (Growing up, Janet and I shared many escapades together not the least of which was smoking for the first time, in her garage, and singing and dancing in her attic to the recordings of Doris Day.)

For all my complaining and wishing to stay home (the mosquitoes, horseflies, cold temperatures, driving rain, long drives to the camp site, Nana fussing about Pop's driving), I do remember I learned that nature has much to teach me about the life cycle certainly, but also about the glories of God's creation at sunrise, at dusk, and the in-between.

I need to buy a boat.

June 23, 2003

"Today I Cried My Eyes Out"

You called me with a terrible head cold, four audition turn-downs, the feeling of having few friends, no sense of the future with your man, no money for insurance, two jobs you hate...

I cried my eyes out that you felt so low. If you ever have a child, you will learn that a parent will do almost anything to take away the child's hurt, except, you can't, because it is her path, her choice, her turn to learn.

June 24, 2003

"Composing"

Last evening I heard an excellent concert in our Weber Music Hall at UMD. Dvorak was followed by Bizet and then an original composition by an alumnus. The concert got me thinking about composing.

When Max composes music, he takes out music paper and writes it down never touching the piano. I have seen him scoring a piece ("scoring" meaning adding the notes for bass, guitar, drums etc.) and never playing it on the piano. He has gone to a gig and heard his orchestration for the first time in rehearsal! When asked, he simply tells me he hears it in his head.
This is a musical gift.

Only once did a tune come to me and I turned it into a "Children's Christmas Carol." I was walking on the shore and I heard a tiny bird sing a melody that stuck with me. I came home and plunked it out on the piano and then wrote it down and added the words. Do you remember it?

Have you, Monette, had a song come to you? If so, write it down. Otherwise it might slip away in the night.

"Just Spell..."

So last evening at Emily's Fish Boil, Pam and Neale joined us for supper. Fortunately for me, we have been friends forever. Neale was in rare form and told the following joke:

A woman died and went to heaven and when she arrived at the pearly gates, an angel met her and said, "You can enter heaven if you can spell the word 'love.' "

The woman spelled "L-O-V-E" and she went into heaven.

Years later when her husband appeared at the gates, she was now in charge. Being so glad to see him, the woman asked, "How have you been?" "Great," he said. "After you died, I married a beautiful woman, we had great sex and a wonderful life, and I won the lottery. Now, how do I get into heaven?"

"No problem," she said. "Just spell Czechoslovakia!"

"Warner"

Last night I dreamt about my brother Warner. When he came home from the Navy looking dashing in his uniform, he showed us movies he had taken aboard his naval ship, the USS *Intrepid*, close to Cuba. Although we teased Warner about his Cuban film (lots of footage of the sea), it was fascinating to realize he actually was that close to Havana and visited Guantanamo Bay four times. (This was when Castro was fighting Batista for power.) While in the Navy he occasionally wrote to me, and I cherished the letters and showed them to my closest girlfriends.

As a kid, I remember being impressed by his scuba diving in Lake Superior, his working on the boats on the Great Lakes, and his majoring in speech therapy in college. Also, he had a great group of friends, some of whom I see in Duluth and elsewhere, to this day. It was Warner who inspired me to attend UMD where we both had the same academic advisor.

As you know, he and Judy, the love of his life, are in Las Vegas. Judy's job as a child psychologist brought them there. When Warner showed us Red Rock Canyon National Conservation Area where he worked, we were blown away by the beauty of the area. This is the natural side of Vegas and more stunning than anything the strip could ever create. Later we loved swimming in their pool and Judy's great steak dinner.

Warner was the first in the family to own (and success-fully operate!) a computer, and he was the first to buy a hybrid car. My big brother is strong, courageous, and quiet. "Still waters run deep."

Warner and Judy took care of Nana at the end of her life for which I will always be grateful. They are very proud of their children, Wendy and Chris, and should be.

Always remember, your aunts and uncles and cousins are there for you, if you need them. And you for them.

"Reading a Good Book is Like Having a Best Friend"

When I am reading a great book, I feel good inside all day knowing I can get back to it at the end of the day. No matter what happens at work, I have a "best friend" to turn to when day is done. Even more than inspired writing, I am a slave to a good story. Of course one hopes to read books that are well written AND tell a tale worth sharing.

You asked me for a list of some of my favorite books. Here are a few:

1. *The Heart is a Lonely Hunter* by Carson McCullers
2. *An American Tragedy* by Theodore Dreiser
3. *Bleak House* by Charles Dickens
4. *The Josephine Bonaparte Trilogy* by Sandra Gulland
5. *Long Walk to Freedom* by Nelson Mandela
6. *Siddhartha* by Hermann Hesse
7. *...And Ladies of the Club* by Helen Hooven Santmyer
8. *Zelda* by Nancy Milford
9. *Gifts from the Sea* by Anne Morrow Lindbergh
10. *Meridian* by Alice Walker
11. *A Fine Balance* by Rohinton Mistry

What are your favorite reads?

"Entertaining"

Everything I learned about entertaining, I learned from Nana. She was an excellent hostess. Company came first. She had a special drawer in the house for company towels and linens. Our house was always "visitor ready." She baked and cleaned and cooked for days beforehand. There were fresh flowers in the summer time, like a large bunch of lilacs. Or a branch from the flowering crab apple tree in the backyard. And Nana featured vegetables from her "Victory Garden" which she explained as a remnant from World War Two. Here were her rules:

1. Offer a drink the moment guests arrive. A glass of wine relaxes a person; therefore, have one yourself before your company arrives.
2. Watch out for Potlucks. Must be ready with each course in case someone doesn't make it. Example: have wine and hors d'oeuvres out even if someone is assigned to them. Dessert people need refrigerator space and everyone needs utensils. Some need to stir, bake, cut or whip their offerings. The kitchen ends up to be the best space for shared work and conversation.
3. Although Nana featured a relish tray (olives, radishes, pickles, stuffed celery, deviled eggs, carrots) and I never do so, I get a lump in my throat when I am offered one at a dinner remembering all those holiday dinners and ladies' luncheons in Lakeside. So consider putting out a relish tray. I am sure no one does so in L.A., but you could start a new trend.
4. When preparing for a dinner, begin at the end with the dessert, and work backwards. By the end you are ready with social hour. (I also do this with menus at restaurants by

eyeing the desserts first and reading back to the appetizers. And this system works if you do the "Jumble" in the news-paper. Just arrange the letters they give you, backwards, and you have an advantage. Dare I also add that any maze goes twice as fast if you start with the end and, again, work backwards. You get the idea.)

5. NEVER try a new recipe on company. And sample the wine beforehand. Three times out of ten, it has gone bad.

"Entertaining" continued...

6. Put out your best magazines like *Architectural Digest*, *The New Yorker*, *Gourmet*. (Nana would put out *Time Magazine*, *Life Magazine* and the *Ladies Home Journal*.)
7. Don't repeat tastes: lemon, olives, cheese, for example. If you use citrus in the salad, use dark chocolate for dessert. Although dark chocolate can be repeated throughout the meal. (smile)
8. Don't keep people longer than 1 hour and 20 minutes at the table. Folks need to move around.
9. Think through possible topics of conversation that might be of mutual interest and let everyone have their say. Draw out the quiet ones. (Politics and religion and abortion and gay rights, as topics, can cause heartburn and spoil your dinner.)
10. Place flowers in the bathroom.
11. Ask your cat to get lost in case of allergies.

The most memorable dinner party we ever hosted was to have nothing but wine and substantial hors d'oeuvres ready when guests arrived and to divide the twelve people into four groups of three, give each group $25 and have them go out and come back with one of the courses (salad and bread, meat/fish, vegetables, dessert.) It was loads of fun and the meal, cooked and assembled in our kitchen, was quite good. (No spouses/partners on the same team.) $25 wouldn't go far today but it sure is nice not to have to cook.

You have Nana's knack for entertaining, Missy. Enjoy!

"Over the Rainbow" (by Harold Arlen and Frank Churchill)

"Somewhere Over the Rainbow
way up high.
There's a land that I heard of
once in a lullaby.
Somewhere Over the Rainbow
skies are blue
And the dreams that you dare
to dream really do come true.
Some day I'll wish upon a star
and wake up where the clouds
are far behind me.
Where troubles melt like lemon
drops a way above the chimney
tops that's where you'll find me.
Somewhere Over the Rainbow
blue birds fly. Birds fly over the
Rainbow. Why, oh why, can't I?"

You frequently ask Max to play this for you. It is such a beautiful song. Ask him to tell you about the lost verse which was only in the British version:
"Once, by a word, only lightly spoken all your dreams are broken for a while.
Sadness comes and joy goes by but every tear like the rain descending finds a happy ending in a smile.
Doubts and tears all fade and die to the blue beyond the grey love again will find its way."
As recorded recently by Bill Bolcom, Joan Morris, Max Morath in
Bolcom, Morris, Morath Sing Yip Harburg.

July 1, 2003

"WHITE RABBIT" you got me!

****

"On Friendship"

Did I remember to tell you that to be invited out, you must invite others in?

When you meet someone you would very much like to get to know better, extend an invitation to meet. You will know immediately during a second interaction if the two of you click.

A new friendship is like a mating game. There is attraction, excitement and energy between you. There is the promise of friendship and the desire to learn something from your new friend. When it goes well, this relationship can grow to trust and the promise of fun and shared experiences. If not, it goes nowhere.

The signs of "going nowhere" can include stifled yawns, boredom, listening only, feeling uncomfortable, and your instinct telling you, "I want out."

If this happens, wish the person well and move on. It's no one's fault.

A real friendship should never be lopsided. It is best when there is give and take and concern for the other. And there is no time clock on friendship. Some last a lifetime and others, a single season. When you reconnect with an old friend, however, it feels like springtime, all fresh but remembered.

Friendships take time and energy. You cannot just collect people like pebbles on the beach to be put in a jar and forgotten. Some friends are related to a time and place, and others to a shared experience and still others, mutual interests and attraction. The bottom line is that your friend makes you feel GOOD about yourself, you enjoy doing something for them and with them, and that there are lessons to learn from this person.

DIANE FAY SKOMARS

I am wondering how you keep in touch with the friends you meet through acting?

July 2, 2003

"A, B, C of Songs"

Whenever we travel, Max and I play the game, the "A, B, C of Songs." Here is how it goes:

I hum a complete song whose title starts with the letter "A." For example, "Around the World I Searched for You." If Max doesn't recognize it, I get a point.

Next, he hums a song with a title beginning with the letter "B." For example, "Beautiful Dreamer." If I don't guess it, he gets a point.

We go through the entire alphabet racking up points. If you play this game, here are some hints:

"Que Sera, Sera" is your best bet for "Q."

"Zip-a-Dee-Doo-Dah" for the letter "Z."

"Until the Real Thing Comes Along" for "U." (Max's favorite)

"Until the Twelfth of Never." (my choice)

When one of us gets behind in points, Max resorts to obscure songs by Irving Berlin and Paul Dresser. I, however, choose from Lutheran hymns or Girl Scout melodies. It is the only way to stump him!

Try it!

"I Sure Miss You"

We live so far apart. Duluth to L. A. might as well be Helsinki to Cape Town. Doesn't seem fair that I only see my girl at Christmas and once or twice in between. Talking by phone most days does help but...

Sometimes I dream we are closer and can meet for tea, knitting, a film date, a Santa Monica beach day complete with a Ferris wheel ride, or a hike.

I sure miss you.

July 4, 2003

"Strawberry Cake"

    1 package white cake mix
    1 package strawberry jello
    1/2 cup water
    3 tablespoons flour
    1 cup oil
    4 eggs
    1 package (10 oz.) frozen strawberries
    Frosting:
    1 pound powdered sugar
    1 stick butter, softened

Mix and beat first six ingredients together. Add half package strawberries slightly thawed. When well mixed, pour into two 8x8 layer pans that have been well greased and floured. Bake 30 minutes at 350 degrees.

Frosting:
Mix sugar and butter together. Add remainder of berries and beat to spreading consistency.

With thanks to friend Connie for this wonderful recipe. (She and Bill are the only two people who see more films than I do! A remarkable, loving couple in so many ways.)

July 5, 2003

"Here's Looking at You"

The camera has always played an important role in my life. Pops had a dark room in the basement and owned more than one camera (including a large Speed Graphic). I was his subject in the early years of my life and the camera was like a sixth member of our family, usually present and ready to record the scene.

I don't remember being posed, but I do remember the click of the shutter and later the excitement of watching the film being processed before my very eyes in the dark room. Pops had an excellent eye, and he was generous. He taught me how to use the camera and how to respect it.

When I won a camera in a contest, I was off and running. My early photographs were grainy and, of course, black and white (which I still prefer). As cameras improved and became easier to handle, my skills improved, and when we moved Out East, I opened a studio of photography.

In our book, *MAX MORATH: The Road to Ragtime*, I write about time in my NY studio: "As I witness the shifting northern light in my studio, I am mindful of the ongoing lessons photography has taught me. They're not about shutter speed and focal length. Rather they are about people. Most people don't like to be photographed and I understand why. The studio is quiet and it's just you and me and the camera, and the camera does not lie. When I light your face, focus the lens, and snap the shutter, I see your essence, your kindness, your humor. It's all there. I don't need special effects - just your honesty and a little luck. That's why I love photography. It is both a skill and an art, and it is by nature a very private business."

You, my dear, helped me set up my studio. You had worked for a photographer in L.A. and guided me with advice on advertising and the business side. You also taught me about photographing actors and, of course, you were my first client. Never will I forget *your* generosity to me. And I will remind you that you inherited Pop's "good eye". Cherish this legacy.

July 6, 2003

"Work is Love Made Visible"

> "Work is love made visible. And if you cannot work with love but only with distaste, it is better that you should leave your work and sit at the gate of the temples and take alms of those who work with joy." Gibran

> I have this quotation on my door at work.

"Heartfelt Apologies"
　　　　"To the men I've loved,
　　　　to the men I've kissed.
　　　　My heartfelt apologies,
　　　　to the men I've missed."
　　　　I found this in Nana's writings. It made me smile.
　　　　And you?

July 8, 2003

Too sad to write today...melancholia.

July 9, 2003

"My Signature Photograph of You on Your 25th Birthday in Florence"

July 10, 2003

"Remembering Our Trip to Italy When You Turned Twenty-Five"

Although I have photographed you all of your life, the one I included yesterday is my favorite. We had arrived in Florence the night before and you were sleeping in until I threw open the shutters to the brilliant sunshine and peeling bells of the morning. You awoke slowly and disappeared to take a shower.

When you came back into the bedroom, your hair was still wet and you were holding a towel around you. You sat by the window and said, "What are we doing today?" I knew I had a magic moment and my trusty 35 Millimeter Minolta did the job.

Your first 25 years flashed in my mind as I took stock of your image; you as a baby child, a toddling toddler, a Girl Scout, a ballerina, a graduate of NYU, a hunter/jumper horse rider, and an actress. But the camera revealed the further truth; you were a woman.

This photograph is my signature piece. And you, my dear, are front and center.

"House Hunting"

We are looking for a house close to campus, to save an hour commute each day, and to get our belongings out of storage. My requirements for a home are:

1. Morning sun must flood the house.
2. We each need an office.
3. The address must have a 4 or 3 in it.
4. It must be very private, hopefully with a fence.

Maxie rolls his eyes at my list and seems to care more about price, taxes, upkeep and how much yard there is to mow.

What are your requirements for a house?

July 12, 2003

WEMAYHAVEFOUNDAHOUSEWEMAYHAVEFOUNDAHOUSEWE-
MAYHAVEFOUNDAHOUSEWEMAYHAVEFOUNDAHOUSEWE-
MAYHAVEFOUNDAHOUSEWEMAYHAVEFOUNDAHOUSEWE-
MAYHAVEFOUNDAHOUSEWEMAYHAVEFOUNDAHOUSEWE-
MAYHAVEFOUNDAHOUSEWEMAYHAVEFOUNDAHOUSE...
WEDIDNOTGETTHEHOUSE...

Handling a keen disappointment is a lesson I am still learning. One can pretend you never wanted it, cry, or decide it was never
meant to be. It also teaches you to never, ever count on anything
for sure. Instead, hold a little optimism back for the possibility of
disappointment.

After all the auditions you have had that went well, seemed
hopeful and yet turned out negative, you must have a handle on
disappointment by now. Perhaps you would be willing to teach me
this lesson.

"Pets"

I grew up with pets. They are such a comfort. First there was Heather, a Scotty dog, who was my brothers' consolation prize when I turned out to be a girl. Since Warner and Buzz were about seven and six at the time, Heather was more their dog. My first cat was named "Dingbat." She tolerated being dressed in baby clothes and going for walks in my doll buggy. Each night Pops would ceremoniously carry Dingbat to the basement and place her in the buggy to sleep. "She likes routine," he'd say. Next came "Ming" and then "Shoo-Shoo," short for "Meshugenah," the latter two being Siamese. I loved them with all my heart.

Although later in life there were dogs (St. Bernard "Ivan" and "Max" the poodle and Llahsa Apso "Bandit" and mutt "Molly"), and your horses, it was the cats that made me happiest. My very best pet came from you, the all white, all male cat, "Foster."

Foster took no prisoners. Dead mice and rabbits appeared at our doorstep compliments of Foster. He prowled by night, but loved to be held like a baby in the morning. He was beautiful and could walk on top of a snowdrift and not fall in. He played "fetch" and could scare a raccoon into believing it was Foster's territory.

Foster got off in Kenosha, WI when we were on our way to NY. Escaping from a harness and the car, he never looked back. We looked for Foster for twenty-four hours but no luck. I cried for a week. We submitted ads to the newspaper. Still miss him, (but don't tell Esme).

Which pet did you love the best?

DIANE FAY SKOMARS

"You Have a Right to Be Here"

"You are a child of the universe no less than the trees and the stars; you have a right to be here. And whether or not it is clear to you, no doubt the universe is unfolding as it should."

Max Ehrmann

I love this quotation. I found it in my daily readings from *The Promise of a New Day,* Hazelden Meditations, by Karen Casey and Martha Vanceburg. I keep it in my planner for the times I go dark inside and feel like I am disappearing. To me it means that I, too, have the right to exist and to stand firm like the trees and to sparkle like the stars.

The trick to this thinking is to figure out how we can be so small, so insignificant and so forgotten in the vast universe, and at the same time believe that one person can actually make a difference and impact the world.

The quotation is from *Desiderata: Words for Life.* Are you familiar with this poem? If not, stop right now and look it up and read it. It is remarkable.

July 15, 2003

"Affirmation to Forgive"

"I forgive you completely and freely. I release you and let you go.

So far as I'm concerned, the incident that happened between us is finished forever.

I wish the best for you. I wish for you your highest good. I hold you in the light.

I am free and you are free, and all again is well between us.

Peace be with you."

Connie Domino, *The Law of Forgiveness*

Last year I picked this up at your church, All Saints, in Pasadena. I keep a copy with me just in case I need it.

July 16, 2003

"Salade"

Baby spinach
Sliced mushrooms
Chopped walnuts
Dressing:
3 Tablespoons mayonnaise
2 Tablespoons Dijon mustard
1 Tablespoon yellow mustard
3 Tablespoons red wine vinegar
1 teaspoon fresh tarragon
pepper and salt to taste
salad oil (enough to make it creamy-like)

Mix above ingredients, adding oil SLOWLY while stirring. I
had this recipe in Arizona at a friend's home and loved it!

July 17, 2003

"House Negotiations"

They said $233,000.

We said $215,000.

They said $230,000.

We said $220,000.

They said $227,000.

We said $225,000, final answer.

They said...pause..."ok."

These negotiations on a house deal must seem strange to you in L.A. where buyers often pay MORE than the asking price and houses start at $850,000. However, the concept is the same. We could be firm about the price because we had some doubts and because we had a bottom line.

Lesson: Always know your bottom line and don't budge when there are doubts.

"Admit No Negative Thoughts"
Maxie Taxi taught me his favorite mantra today. Note the changing emphasis.

Admit no negative thoughts.
Admit *no* negative thoughts.
Admit no *negative* thoughts.
Admit no negative *thoughts.*
Admit no negative thoughts.
Admit *no* negative thoughts.
Admit no *negative* thoughts.
Admit no negative *thoughts.*
Admit no negative thoughts.
Admit *no* negative thoughts.

What do you use as your mantra when you cannot sleep?

July 19, 2003

"Foxes"

Yesterday I dropped Max off at the airport early, early. It was Sunday so rather quiet in Beautiful Duluth. I drove to Park Hill Cemetery to trim Nana and Pop's gravesite.

There, before my eyes, were two darling foxes chasing each other between head stones. Although I was out of the car and watching their every move, they paid me no never mind. They hid, spied, and then ran toward the other taking cover behind trees and markers. It was a joy to behold their merry chase.

It gave me such comfort to know that foxes play where Nana and Pops rest.

You already know that I have a plot at Park Hill Cemetery next to Nana and Pops, and my gravestone is in place. (Add no dates, please.) Cremation will do. I will NOT ask you to visit my grave often because I know you will never reside in Duluth, Minnesota. You will find the cemetery a peaceful place near a pond with ducks and high-flying geese. If you come, you will feel a connection to family and the good earth. We thank you, in advance, for dropping by.

DIANE FAY SKOMARS

July 20, 2003

"Memorial"
I might as well complete this talk of my demise. A memorial service at First Lutheran Church in Duluth would be good. Please ask the organist to play it full and with gusto! They will want only Lutheran hymns played but try to slip in "Finlandia" and "It's a Wonderful World" by Louis Armstrong and Max's recording of "Let It Alone" and "Brother, Can You Spare a Dime?" I believe Lucy would help you with details and Jeanne with music. (Maybe she would do a violin solo, dark Finnish music.) A reception/lunch after at a restaurant or club featuring Finnish vodka and *good* food seems fitting. No passing the mic.

Keep the service short but do include communion. One hour twenty. Do not create one of those boards with "snap shots." Just use the painting by Bela Petheo. Ashes could be in a wooden box that Scott might be willing to make, or in the covered ceramic Christmas grog pitcher. I know you hate this stuff but there you are. (A few of the ashes could be scattered in Finland by you and Mia.) Any gifts could go to the UMD Women's Hockey Scholarship, UMD Skomars Family Scholarship, the UMD FinnFest Scholarship or any other UMD scholarship. Bury me privately earlier that same morning. Remember, I gave you the list of favorite hymns.

Thank you for sending me off...

"Turning Over Personal Power"

I have allowed someone I know bother me. I view her as a strong woman with a sharp tongue that could potentially harm me. Even though my brain tells me I am giving her too much power, my feelings remind me of the threat. Am uneasy around her but have never told her. Need to know what is behind this and am I making this up? My NY therapist always told me to go with my instincts.

One would think that at age 60, I would be free of this nonsense. Plan to talk to her this afternoon...

Later: I found out that she feels the same way about me and, in fact, uses her snappish ways for protection. Gulp! In the meantime, things have eased between us and we have dropped some of our defenses. Glad we talked. We will never be close friends, but we are closer for our conversation.

Lesson: whenever you have a problem with someone - go to that person directly and talk it through.

July 22, 2003

"The Inspector"

The house inspector stood on the roof of "our" house and announced for all to hear:

"This won't do! I see cracks in the shingles here and cracks in the shingles there. I see 30-40 cracks in the shingles! This is not good! I will now take photographs of the shingles for you to see. It can only get worse."

We slept on this news, rather, didn't sleep. Pop's words rang in my head: "Never compromise on a roof. It is the umbrella of the house."

Decision: we let the house go.

"Yahtzee Central"

I found these sketches from the last time we three had a Yahtzee tournament. It is easy to see who won each round.

"Hiking"

Max and I hiked deep into the woods up the shore. In the final 45 minutes, there was almost no trail left - all overgrown. On the way up we saw a couple with open toes and no water bottles. We knew they would turn around soon, and sure enough, they did.

When you hike into the woods always bring: hiking boots, hat, long sleeves and long pants, bug spray, sun tan lotion, water, compass, power bars, and "ten cents to call home." This was a joke in my family. Nana always sent a dime with me when I ventured into the forest with the Girl Scouts. "But, *Mom*, there are no phones in the woods!" I'd exclaim. "Nevertheless, take the dime," she'd counter.

Are you a hiker in Pasadena? If so, where do you go and what are you looking for?

"The Clock is Ticking"

I hate it when the elders are correct. For example, they say time goes by faster and faster the older one gets. And, indeed, it does.

Act One, Ages 0-30
"You're in anticipation of what is to come."
Act Two, Ages 30-60
"You're absorbed in what has come."
Act Three, Ages 60-90
"You're reflecting on what became of your life."

Maxie has a theory about this matter. He believes that when you are born you have your entire life before you. Therefore, time stretches and the future seems endless.

When you are in middle age, you have only half your life left so time speeds up.

And when you are older, there is less time left in this life and time just flies by. It is all about *your* perspective, but Max's theory makes sense to me.

What do you believe?

"In Anticipation"

Today I am like a child because I am "in anticipation" of my visit to you. Since first grade I have been going to Southern California for fun. First, Aunt Effie and Aunt Fay lived there; then Pat and Buzz; next Nana and Pops; now you!

I simply cannot wait to see you. As my friend Judith once said about her grown son, "I just like to be close enough to occasionally smell his shampoo!" Mothers understand such a statement. I come to smell your shampoo, My Dear.

July 27, 2003

"I Am With You"

Since I arrived in L. A., you and I have been on the go. Difficult to find time to write without your knowing about it.

Yesterday when we shopped separately at T J Max, we selected the exact same items, as usual. All your life, we have shared the same taste when selecting gifts and such. It is uncanny. Are there shopping genes?

It is grand to be with you!

"Too Busy"

Too busy having fun with you to write.

Lesson: it is okay to let go of the "duty" occasionally and just be in the moment and have some fun!

July 29, 2003

"Agents"

I love it that you have an agent, Sheldon has an agent, and his HOUSE in Pasadena has an agent. It is a perfect double-story, all-American house with "good bones."

I also love it that the house receives the profits from the commercials that are booked here. A new chimney, mended fence and art pieces for the house are the rewards for "posing."

It is so good to be with you! L. A. is a trip.

"A Jewel of a Girl"

You showed me your new jewelry web site: www.hollywood-rosejewelry.com

As I travel to foreign lands, I enjoy searching for antique pins. You turn them into wearable art and they in turn carry within them the hands of the original creator, the wearer, you the artist and finally the new owner. Appreciating the journey of your creations is a key to your success.

How did you get started making jewelry and when did you begin incorporating old brooches and the like? I don't remember. I do remember that artistic endeavors were in your makeup.

Thank you for remembering your Momma with your lovely pieces of art. It never fails: when I wear your jewelry, someone always asks, "Where did you get that necklace?" And I send them straight to your web site.

What other mother can contact her daughter with: "I need a show-stopping piece to go with a new mauve dress?" Voila! The package arrives.

July 31, 2003

"The Lesson of Venice"

I am thinking again about our trip to Italy when you were 25. We wove our way around Venice wheeling our bags, got to our hotel room and crashed. We had hauled our heavy suitcases up three flights and were worn out. You fell asleep, and I lay on my bed with the shutter flung open wide. Because we faced an inner courtyard, I could hear the sounds of cooking and the smell of pasta sauce simmering. I also overheard family members arriving at the apartment across from us. The meal proceeded with lots of laughter and stories in Italian, with food being passed. It sounded delicious to me.

Tears streamed down my cheeks and I was hungry for family, for gatherings for meals, for laughter and good times, for stories of the past. It brought back memories of wonderful pot-lucks up the shore with my grandmother, lots of great cousins (especially Myrna, Janice and Betty), uncles, aunts and, of course, the five of us in my family. There were stories, jokes, horseshoes, and a picnic (homemade potato salad, chicken, ham, bread, jello, fresh blueberry pies) and card games after my Grandma Skomars took a nap. I always believed the story that my first words were, "Shut up and deal."

Later I told my therapist about the Venice scene and she said, "Don't be ridiculous! Some of them probably hate each other and were just being polite because their grandmother was present." We had a good laugh.

So, my dear, understand what you are missing in your life, but don't ever believe others have it made.

D I A N E   F A Y   S K O M A R S

"WHITE RABBIT!!!" We got each other.

****

Photograph from the Trevi Fountain, Rome, 1999

"Here Are Some Questions I Have Always Wanted to Ask You."

Is acting escaping from real life or is it explaining real life to you?

Are you in theatre because you like to become someone else or for the applause?

What do you admire in other actors? What do they admire in you?

Does your agent work hard for you every day?

What advice do you give newly arrived actors to L.A.?

Does everyone prepare as hard as you do for an audition or a role?

Why do you wear the same thing to the audition when you are called back?

What do you do when you strongly disagree with a director's interpretation of your role?

What role did you love the most?

Can you ever just enjoy the run of a show and not be pitching for the next job?

Is it true that only 4 % of all actors are working at any given time?

Do actors make good friends? Are actors generous people?

Where did "break a leg" come from?

If you weren't an actor, what would you do? (I can hear you now, "Never ask me that question, Mother!")

"Go Out Sailing"

By the time you read this entry you won't remember that I told you today about two stories of elders who "retired."

The first was a gentleman who, when his wife died, declared to his family that he was selling everything (yes, they could have what they wanted in the house) and moving to Paris and living in a modest apartment. He would spend the rest of his life sipping coffee or schnapps on a tree-lined boulevard, reading the *International Herald*, and playing chess. Anyone who cared to visit could, and he would put them up in a nearby hotel for a week and be glad for their company. You see, he had observed that Europe was kinder to seniors than they were in Omaha. And he never had to drive again or linger in a home for the aged.

The second story I love is about the woman who retired aboard an ocean liner. She, too, declared her intentions to her family. It was perfect and less expensive than a home for the aged. And so she circled the globe for years enjoying good food, good company and frequent stops in fascinating ports. She let her family know when she would dock near them in case they had time to visit, and she offered each member a free Atlantic crossing each year on her vessel.

Be prepared!

"Roses at Rose's"

Today I trimmed your rose bushes and loved it. I am amazed at your many talents:

gardener

artist

actress

chef

teacher

You do it all so well.

When you were little you were called Mosie, Rosie, Posie, and just Rose. I love nicknames, do you?

Always take time to smell the roses, Rose.

"S'Mores"

Last evening you and Sheldon and I dined at The Parkway Grille. What a surprise to have gourmet "S'Mores" arrive for dessert. As we ate in style in Pasadena, northern Minnesota came to mind.

As a Girl Scout, I would burn my marshmallow to a crisp and separate the outside shell to reveal the small sweet remains. The chocolate would barely melt between the thick graham crackers. Some part of my "S'More" would inevitably fall to the ground and we would worry all night about the bear who loved dessert.

When you see "comfort food" on a fancy menu, it will often be the best item because chefs had childhoods, too, and will work to recapture those sweet times.

August 6, 2003

"Laramie Project"

Today I read your script and sobbed at the end. The father's speech is so very moving. "He was not alone"...

How could it have happened? A young man beaten into a coma state in 1998, tied to a fence in a field in Wyoming, and left to die in freezing weather. All because he was gay.

Your association with this project says a lot about you, your talents and your values. I am so proud of you, Monette.

With the real issues in life (hunger, homelessness, war, abuse), I cannot imagine people meddling in others' lives, or abusing them about sexual preference.

I ask you to explain to me: what are people afraid of to become so violent?

"Fly Away from LA to NY"

It still astounds me that we can fly across country having had breakfast with a one loved in Pasadena and dinner with another in Manhattan. We have come to expect this phenomenon as our-right-to-flight. And because nearly everyone flies now, the skies are filled with planes crisscrossing the atmosphere in patterns never before imagined. Pilots are on autopilot, the stewards too busy to assist a crying baby or a gentleman with heartburn, and the once consumable meals are downgraded or not offered at all.

We all want to get there in a hurry, and there is a price. Looking ahead, I wonder if we will one day be offered flights of speed versus flights of fancy in which we don't use fossil fuel and we take a plane that hovers over the Grand Canyon and grand cities of our time and has a glass bottom for passenger-viewing of the great sites of the world. In other words, we take our time...from the air.

The seating can be in circles with a chef in the middle, and because we can walk around, we can interact with the gentleman in 7B or the child in 36A instead of just our seatmate. Oh yes, the spa is on the upper level. On board is a lecturer who has studied Moral Leadership and a violinist prepared to play us into slumber. Stewards are hired and rewarded in the great art of **service**. They know our names and our desires. The introverts are in one circle, left alone to read or listen to recorded books or music. Members of AA can gather in the meeting room. And the children can learn about iguanas in the petting zoo, lower level. All seats tilt back for comfortable sleeping.

Impossible? Not really. In Nana's lifetime, a man first flew across the Atlantic Ocean in 1927. And in mine, we landed on the moon in 1969. In your lifetime, I am suggesting an airline that does not offer "faster and farther" but "slower and more pleasurable."

Advice: when you next take a ride by air, exhausted from the security scrutiny and claustrophobic from the over-booking, let your mind float on my ideas plus your own. You can escape to what's possible...

August 8, 2003

"New York, New York"

I had breakfast with friend Donna, and then Max and I picked up our rental truck and drove through the Lincoln Tunnel to Michael and Christy's where we had a wonderful dinner on their deck.

Moving the rest of our belongings from NY to Duluth is a daunting experience. You would think by now I could have shed more things knowing a large heap of boxes will again get stored for years in a garage or storage unit. I just cannot give up my favorite cowgirl boots, sheet music from my piano bench, Pop's slides of our family, or your baby blanket. Entire books have been written about the clutter in our lives and yet, I simply cannot let go of these boxes because they contain remnants of my life and yours.

I have read that we can more easily let go of our stuff if we give most away and not throw it out. Somehow, the fact that someone else may benefit from the treasure eases our minds about parting with it.

And so my boxes will once again get moved.

What do you do with "remnants" of *your* life?

Are you a saver or a thrower?

August 9, 2003

"Ask Me What I Think of U-Haul"

Max and I drove back into the city and it took four men four hours to pack the truck. We began the drive. All was going well until, while we were driving in the rain in upper NY State, the truck stopped dead! Tried to reach U-Haul using their 800 number but were put on hold. Because we were holding up traffic and stuck in the middle of the highway, the sweet State Highway Patrol Officer wanted us off the road A.S.A.P. Several hours and $297 later, we were towed to a U-Haul garage in the next town. Cripes!

Here is what I learned today: when your truck stalls on a freeway in the rain, keep your husband from getting out of the cab; put on your blinkers; get on the phone; be polite to the highway patrol because they can call the tow truck folks; chew gum; be glad you have a roll of twenties; freshen up your make-up because you will be interacting with a lot of strangers who can help you (or not); understand it is not life or death; sing "We Shall Overcome."

"Freaky Friday"

Got stuck for the weekend because the mechanic that specializes in fixing U-Haul trucks, was fishing. We cut our losses and rented a small vehicle and drove to the Hudson River for a boat cruise and a movie, *Freaky Friday.*

Remember: when you cut your losses, always plan something fun to replace the disappointment. It helps.

August 11, 2003

"Starting to Get Funny"

George, who had been fishing and was the only "authorized" U-Haul mechanic, showed up with a friend and after hours of probing, declared it was the starter and battery and replaced both. U-Haul would not pay so our personal charges went sky high. But we were on our way again. By now I am worried about getting back to work on time.

Later in the day, we were stalled out AGAIN (still in NY state!) and had the new "bad" battery replaced AGAIN and the charges grew. Yikes!

What do you do with bad news upon bad news? At a certain point, I seem to go inside and get the giggles. I find it funny to realize I don't even know what town we are in, who to believe when they diagnose "the problem," and why I thought a roll of twenties would help us on the road! These are the times you think your marriage will be tested but instead, you become a team of "you and me against the world," and you play good cop/bad cop, and help your mate who might be losing faith.

This whole episode is also a reminder that although we have four degrees between us, enough money to ordinarily roll along, and profound belief that we are guided by our Creator, there is not one thing we can do to change the fact that our &*%$#*@# U-Haul truck continues to stop dead in its tracks!!! So we might as well laugh.

DIANE FAY SKOMARS

"Ohio"

The Ohio Turnpike was the next trouble spot for us. We knew the drill. Put on flashers and try to pull over as the motor conks out. Stay in the truck. Call U-Haul's 800 number and pray you get a REAL person who doesn't put you on hold. Lisa is our savior and promises action. Sure enough, the wrecker/tow truck showed up and hauled us to Sandusky, an hour away. We learned the wrecker itself costs $200,000 and has 13 forward gears and we were with a pro at last. Max rode shotgun and I was in the bunk. Finally, some fun and perhaps, a solution.

I tell you all this so you will know what to do when confronted with a breakdown of any kind: 1. Follow instructions only when helpful. 2. Put your safety first. 3. Go with the pro. 4. Find the humor. 5. Keep a written, running log of date, time, place, and details. 6. Remember, your money is meant to be spent for your comfort and safety when there is trouble.

August 13, 2003

"Sleepless in Sandusky"

After talking half the night, Max and I decided I needed to go to the nearest airport and fly home to get back for work. I ordered a car to pick me up. Hated to leave the Max with the drive but we had to assume the truck was fixed at last.

The only car available was a white stretch limo so I arrived at the Cleveland Airport in style, exhausted, but in style. By now paying for a limo and a last minute plane ticket seemed normal, to say nothing of the last U-Haul makeovers.

Remember when I told you about doing your own packing and moving? Forget it! Call the nearest movers and let them do it all.

DIANE FAY SKOMARS

"Moving On"

Max is on the road alone with the truck that seems to be fixed at last!

Looking back I would say that persistence and friendliness paid off the most. My initial spouting and pouting and demonstrated anger did not yield good results. Maxie taught me how to cope, accept and move on (of course not in the truck, just in the mind!). Glad we aren't dead or injured.

U-Haul needs to overhaul their breakdown communication system. We will be submitting our complaints.

Trust everyone but keep the receipts.

August 15, 2003

"Reading"

I remember the summer you gave up reading. You declared, at age six, you were tired of it and done with it. Waiting for it to change, I finally realized you meant it. Remembering how you always wanted to buy comic books, I gave you money to do so. Somehow you didn't equate comic books with reading. That summer you must have read four-dozen comic books. When school started you were back reading books.

Do you remember the summer you gave up on books? If so, do you remember why?

August 16, 2003

"Christmas in August"

It is very hot here, even by the big lake. Waiting for the wind to shift from the Northeast.

I am going over my Christmas gifts already purchased for over twenty people.

When I asked my NY therapist about my need to buy so many gifts, she said, "Why not?" When I asked her how to select a gift for someone else, she said it was not what the person needed or wanted or what you had on hand, but rather, "Buy a gift that says how you feel about the person."

Remember the time I bought you an electronic keyboard for Christmas? You cried and told me the gift was what I would want for you not what you would want. Gulp! Fortunately I saved the receipt and we returned it and you bought black leather pants. Am not sure what my therapist would say about this story.

Lesson: in the case of daughters, it is best to buy them what they *want*.

"It's Never Too Late"

Am so glad you are here! Not much time to write plus I don't want to get caught writing since this project is your surprise Christmas gift. But I do want to share these thoughts.

I heard on public radio that parents are poor at teaching their young about how to handle the bad times. Gulp! I believe this is true. I think I was a distractor, a soother, a "let me kiss your owie" type. The "right way," currently, is to acknowledge a child's minor pain or upset and ask them to put into words the situation and help *them* figure out how to turn things around.

I think I was a mother cat trying to soothe the way for you and helping you avoid trouble; also I was ready to pounce on anyone who hurt you. But maybe it isn't too late for both of us to learn how to handle the bad times.

When the world truly rains on your parade, try facing it head-on. That's right, look your troubles in the eye, wallow in them, cry a river over them, and when you are spent,

1. Take an aspirin, Tums and a bubble bath.
2. Go to bed and write about your troubles.
3. Then put on a recording of Peggy Lee's "Is That All There Is?" and have a hot fudge sundae.
4. Go to the humane society and order two cats and name one Laurel and the other Hardy.
5. Finally, call a friend with worse troubles and take her out for lunch.

"Take a Hike"

We went hiking in Gooseberry State Park today. You loved the waterfalls but not the bugs and the woods...same as when you were little. Hard to convince you about the beauty of the "great out-of-doors" when you are miserable with mosquito bites. Calamine lotion still helps.

Remember the time you went to camp for the first time at about age 7? It was a week long program in the woods in northern Minnesota. Two days after we left you at camp, you sent a post card with the following note:

"Get me out of here!!!"

I called the Director and told her, "I am not telling you what to do, just that we received the card." She laughed and said you had found a best friend and hoped to return to camp next year.

Lesson: don't judge anything by the first day or anyone by the first meeting. Give it time.

August 19, 2003

"One Real Fight"

You were charming at the Vanilla Bean Cafe in Two Harbors. Friends Jan and Paul prepared a wonderful Tuscan meal for you and our guests. Still can't believe you are here.

You selected the menu from Jan's suggestions. You always have been a "take charge" person when called upon. I like that trait in you although once it didn't work.

I remember only one real fight with you, when you were 16 years of age. You challenged me and swore at me. It was a tense time in the garage in Columbia, MO. Hating discord in any form, I usually would go along but this time I stood my ground and said "no." I told you I was leaving because you were disrespecting me and had to cool down. I turned my back and went into the house. Later you apologized.

I cannot tell you what our fight was about. The car? A purchase? A curfew? Do you even remember this?

Tonight, as I looked at you speaking with ease to our friends and relatives, I remembered our good times together all your growing-up years. The drives to the horse barn, your after-school visits to my office at Stephens College, our trips to see Nana and Pops, the overnights with the Girl Scout Troop, the cabin in Wisconsin, shopping at the Kansas City Plaza. It is a joyful memory all rolled into one good feeling of love.

My thought for you today is to cherish each day for itself and let the good accumulate over time to get you through the tough times.

"Outside the Box"

You asked me where I got the notion to come up with seven solutions for every major problem. I got it from the idea that one can solve problems by expanding the possibilities for solutions and by thinking outside the box. Here are examples of what is meant, the kind of thinking I admire.

Problem: a truck was 2 inches too tall to go through a mountain tunnel.
Solution: the driver let air out of the tires and drove through the tunnel.

Problem: a recent widow didn't have the strength to turn the bed mattress to correct the two sagging sides.
Solution: she began sleeping in the middle of the bed to even out the mattress.

Problem: residents in an apartment building in Paris complained to the "super" that the elevator was too slow. There was no money for a new one.
Solution: the "super" installed a lovely mirror in the elevator and there were no more complaints.

In the first example, most drivers would have turned around and lost valuable time. In the second, it would have made sense to simply order a new mattress or at least hire someone to turn the old one. She saved money and had the satisfaction of solving it herself. I love the third example because it required knowing human nature and therein lies the key.

Never come up with only one solution and always think outside the box.

"A Working Single Mom"

    I tried hard to drive you to the Twin Cities today but work interfered. I tried not to recall all the events I missed in your life because of my job. All those years, work usually came first, gulp! A mother's guilt. I sure felt badly.

    When I told you I couldn't drive you, you were kind. "But Mom, I didn't come on the weekend, when you were free." It helped but I started thinking about years ago.

    Working single moms have an angel on their shoulder because they are not allowed to get sick, get into an accident, or have a bad day. These moms always put their children first and that is where their time and resources go. After a demanding day at work, single mothers arrange for their kids' transportation from school, rush to buy groceries, arrange for lessons, supervise home-work, and cook some kind of meal. They heal wounds of the heart and scrapes of the skin. They have been known to stay up half the night to sew a Halloween costume or care for a sick puppy.

    And they carry around their guilt. The guilt of a failed marriage. The guilt of not having a man's constant good influence on their child in their home. The guilt of not recording her child's illnesses or keeping up the baby book with photographs and cute first words. And the guilt of missing the school play.

    The media comes out with another report on children raised by single parents. Your heart stops until you realize they just said that such a child probably does better with one parent than in a house of real discord.

    The angel on the shoulder of the single working mother doesn't just give out energy and patience and compassion. She spreads her wings and gives these moms extra love for their child. And the relationship that is between the child and the mom is extraordinary. It is because it is "you and me" and we'd better get along and help each other.

    This is just one reason we are close, my dear.

August 22, 2003

"Too sad to write."

I know I am supposed to tell you about my sadness and how I work to get out of it. Mostly it comes from absorbing too much negativity in my heart and not speaking up enough to release it.

I don't think this is your problem, Mosie. You seem to verbalize your feelings at the moment. Good for you. You will be healthier for it.

"Decor"

Today I am remembering the weekend your best friend Mariko and I pulled up the carpeting in our New Jersey house in order to uncover lovely hardwood flooring. It was grueling work, but it did get me thinking about the rules for decorating:

First, the word is draperies, not drapes. (I never use them.)

Second, all pictures should be hung at your eye level except when you are doing a cluster, and even then the primary piece should be at eye level.

Third, think of all surfaces as having art potential. For example, a rug on the floor can be the centerpiece of the room. Or an ancient canoe can be hung from the ceiling. Or a tree can grow indoors in a room with a skylight. Or a room can be empty except for mirrors everywhere.

Fourth, make sure the room has two sources of natural light, if possible.

Fifth, create a conversation circle in the living room where the seating is close and not across the room.

Sixth, keep things off balance. For example, if you have three objects of art on the your mantel, put two to the right and one to the left.

Seventh, a couch and a tall narrow table behind it can break up any room.

Eighth, no personal portraits in the living room. Limit plants to healthy and few.

Ninth, square off chairs and couches to the walls. Never angle furniture.

Tenth, paint now comes in colors to soothe, excite, enhance, soften, startle, create, compliment, contrast and just plain get your engine started! No longer is every room painted "off white." Paint colors can inexpensively change your house and your life. Try it.

Anything goes! I learned all this from Carolyn, Jean, Marilyn, plus two talented decorators.

August 24, 2003

"Lutheran Church"

A wonderful church service today. The minister asked why we were there.

Not because we *should* be there, she said, because we should be cleaning out the garage.

Some may come to meet friends or simply out of habit. Mostly, she said, we come because we are in need of forgiveness. This thought stayed with me all day as I brought up the things I have done wrong in my life. Gulp!

Do you ever go there? How do you handle your list of "wrongs?"

One of my friends sends up a large balloon each year with a list of "wrongs' written on the balloon. It is launched on Park Point and flies over the lake until it disappears. My friend says it is a release of her "sins." (The environmentalists would not approve of the Mylar in the atmosphere.)

I have the hardest time forgiving myself for past deeds. I wonder how I could have been so stupid, so thoughtless, so naive, so quick to anger, and so quick to judge, so dishonest. For me forgiveness comes from identifying the fault, owning it, and getting on my knees. It also requires my attempting to make it right with the person I slighted, hurt or otherwise injured.

It's funny because the "recipient" of my bad manners, after I asked for forgiveness, often says, "Don't be silly. That's not how I took your comment." But at least I can sleep.

Lately I have been aware of my competitive nature that hurries to get in line ahead of another, races to finish first and seeks to do better than others in a contest of any kind. How dumb is this? Am slowing up a bit to make sure that others are accommodated before me.

The lesson: identify past deeds of shame. Seek forgiveness. Forgive self.

"Perpetual Motion"

When you were a toddler, you were in perpetual motion. I used to have to take your photograph in order to see your sweet face. You were such a happy bug, full of life and sunshine and love. Always "busy" with activities, making plans, organizing your room, which was generally orderly.

You had naturally wavy hair and you were a beautiful child. Fearless, curious, and tireless. You loved the arts, animals, and always had one best friend. Loyalty and fairness were keys to your childhood. You were fiercely loyal and showed anger only when "That's not fair!"

When other children were around, you often took a leadership role and organized them in a game, or created a play, or read to them. And you were funny, very funny. You loved hide and seek and laughed a lot.

Now when you are onstage and have a humorous role, I always go back to your essence as an *enfant comique*.

"We are all here for a spell. Get all the good laughs you can." Will Rogers

Once in a while (about twice a year), I collapse into laughter. Tears roll down my cheek. I don't chuckle, I roar, and I lose it. It is embarrassing in a restaurant but there it is. After it is over and I have mopped up, I feel spent and good, sort of like cleaning house. This kind of outburst in me surely releases months of polite talk, holding in feelings, and being nice.

Did you know that jokes are often based on pain? Jokes are usually about some*one*, a stereotype, or an incident that causes hurt. Jokes can be damaging and should be used sparingly. But a funny story can just wipe me out.

Once, I told a friend I heard about a dog that barked once for "yes" and twice for "no" when he was asked a question. I went on to tell my friend that I went straight home and asked cat Esme to blink twice if she understood me. Esme's answer was to turn her head away from me and looked straight at the ceiling as if to say, "You've got to be kidding!" My cat's response was the same no matter how many times I repeated the request. My friend thought it was hilarious that I had tested Esme, and we both started laughing, and laughing. We simply couldn't stop. This, at a public event, with eyes on us. We cannot bring up this subject to this day without laughing.

When you began cooking in earnest, I gave you a plaque for the kitchen with the saying: "Many people have eaten my cooking and gone on to lead normal lives." You told me later, you didn't appreciate it. I, however, thought it was hilarious and I still have it in my kitchen. When I see it, I smile, but I also remember that it hurt you which I *never* intended since you are in fact an excellent cook.

When did you last have a good belly laugh?

August 27, 2003

"Hello Dolly Bars"

8x8 pan
one stick butter melted in pan
layer over the butter, one cup graham cracker crumbs
Add in layers:
1 cup chopped walnuts
1 cup coconut
1 cup chocolate chips (I add butterscotch chips also)
1 can of Eagle Brand Milk (I usually add another 1/2 can)

Do not mix. 1/2 hour at 350 degrees. A crowd pleaser. Thank you, friend Connie, for this recipe.

Always remember that a shared recipe is more about friend-ship than good eating.

DIANE FAY SKOMARS

August 28, 2003

"Buzz's Birthday"

Growing up with two brothers years older than me, my memories include thinking of myself as very small in this household of tall people. Brother Buzz's gift to me was to take me on his paper route (I received a dime each time for my effort), to give me rides on the back of his motorcycle (I still love motor cycles), and to show he cared for me, not in a demonstrative way but in a steady, quiet way. Because of his adventurous spirit, Buzz also taught me that there is life beyond Duluth.

It impressed me that my brother always had a job and always had his own money. At age 16, Buzz and his best friend drove to the state of Washington and picked apples with the migrant workers. After not hearing from him for weeks, we finally received a post card. I remember Nana got on her knees and wept for joy! Buzz was a terrific hockey player and later a stock car racer. When he attended higher education in Minneapolis, he once drove home to Duluth on his motorcycle in a blizzard!!! We had to thaw him out and, once again, Nana wept for joy at his arrival.

Buzz married his high school sweetheart, Patty, and they have two great sons, Scott and Dan, as you know. When Patty was a legal secretary in Duluth and I worked at Wahl's Department Store, we used to meet for lunch or supper. She gave me many of her cast off, high-style clothes for which I was grateful, and I wore them for years. They moved to Australia for over a decade where Buzz worked in Alice Springs. (Isn't it unusual for a family from Duluth to have such strong ties to Australia? Remember that Nana and Pops lived in Tasmania, Australia for five years.)

My brother can fix anything, take an engine apart and put it back together, and remodel a room on a weekend. Not only is he an electrical engineer but a plumber, builder, and carpet installer as well. And he is an exceptional financial manager. Regretfully, I missed that gene. In our youth Buzz often called me "brat" but I knew better. And he was my anchor on 9/11 which I will never forget. It was his steady voice of concern and advice that gave me hope.

"Wish I Was a *Real* Writer"

I must admit that facing an empty page each day is very hard work. I believe I would rather be having a root canal. I imagine that a *real* writer views the blank paper as a kind of canvas in which to paint a picture of truth, revelation or inspiration. I face it as a promise to keep.

When you get to this page in your reading, Monette, you will realize your mother is quite ordinary, uninspiring, and unquotable. That is because I am not a *real* writer who lives to write and, in fact, must write. I am a dabbler who has a few original thoughts and struggles to get them down.

Have I taught you everything I know? I sure hope so because it was the only thing I worried about that fateful day on 9/11. I guess I would like to know if YOU learned anything from these pages or had I already communicated these lessons earlier? Also I would like to know where YOU disagree with me in this journal and where you agree.

One of my problems right now is that there is no one to dialogue with and I am not at all sure of myself as seen through this writing. But I promised to attempt such a journey and I only have September, October, November and December left to create!

I do know you are a *real* writer and I hope you will some day focus on the written page. And truthfully, I have enjoyed writing to you especially on days when there is something worth saying and my life is in focus.

August 30, 2003

"The Academic Cycle"

I have attended many academic events that herald the onset of autumn and the beginning of the school year. Since kindergarten, I have been on the academic cycle.

Fall meant a new plaid skirt and matching sweater or better yet, hand-me-downs from my dear cousins, Myrna and Janice. It meant sharpened pencils, a new notebook and a box of crayons. It meant the beginning of a new year.

Of course you cannot live in the North and not acknowledge all the seasons. Winter here meant snowdrifts and cold and bundling up. Spring, when it finally came in June, was marked by apple blossoms and blooming lilacs. You'd think that summer, with its improved weather and time out, would have been my favorite time of year but it wasn't.

I never trusted summer. It is too much! Too much heat, too many violent storms, too much exposed skin, too many expectations to have fun. Up North heat seems to unbalance people and odd things occur in the summer.

So bring on the beginning of my year, autumn. I shall treat myself to a new plaid skirt and matching sweater.

DIANE FAY SKOMARS

"Picture That"

In the eighties Marianne, Carl and I created "The Reunion Of Sisters" program about Finnish-American women and women of Finland. We sponsored a conference in 1986 in the Twin Cities and another in Kuopio, Finland in 1987 in which we focused on the roles of women in the work force and at home, among other topics. We compared and contrasted the lives of the women of Finland and of Finnish-American women. I met the most wonderful women from both countries and some of us are still in touch with one another.

Do you remember that I simply did not have the money to attend the conference in Finland? I was so sad. But you and I got to work and found a photograph of Finnish Laplanders in a circle around a fire. I then cut out a photograph of myself and we pasted it onto the Finnish picture, and put it on the refrigerator. "I can see myself there," I told you. And you said, "Go Mom!!!"

About 10 days before the conference in Kuopio, Marianne called me and told me the Finnish government was paying our transportation because we were co-chairs. It was magic.

I have used this picture-method three times in my life and it has worked each time. The last time only took 24 hours. If you ever try it, please remember that you must be very serious about *believing* it will come true. Also, keep your passport current at all times.

Do you remember the photograph on the refrigerator and the magic it created?

"WHITE RABBIT!" I got you!

****

"I Will Carry You"

This past week I heard a phrase that went something like this: "If your burdens are great, if you carry much sorrow, if your belief in God is weakening, **I will carry you."**

And once we have received this offer and encouragement from another, we can, in turn, offer it to someone else in need.

I will gladly carry you, knowing you will pass it on.

DIANE FAY SKOMARS

"In Sympathy"

When it comes to expressing sympathy after a death, here are some things to remember.

Use the word "death" or "died" in a card and not "passed" or "passed on."

Recall an incident when you interacted with the deceased and that shows that person in a good light. It can be from a brief interchange and needs to be true. Or if you didn't know the deceased at all, recall something good you heard about her or him.

If appropriate, offer to do something for the person left behind. Be specific. ("I will contact you in a couple of weeks for lunch." "I am happy to help you with writing thank you cards." "We will shovel your walk (or mow your lawn) for the next two weeks." "Call me when you're feeling down; here is my number." "I am happy to drive you for groceries and appointments for one week.")

I like to use the phrase, "In this time of sorrow..."

Include something positive the deceased said to you about the person remaining.

Pay strict attention to the instructions for memorials and send a donation to their designated charity. It matters.

If there is a child in mourning in the family, offer to take that child for a walk and ice cream and just listen.

Bring food over after the service. As my friend says, "The loneliest time is after the funeral when the widow returns to the empty house."

If there was a divorce in this family, reach out to those sometimes excluded in the service. Mourning is shared by all.

September 3, 2003

"Chicago"

I am with Chancellor Martin in Chicago visiting with donors. Chancellor invited me to a viewing of outdoor art renderings for our new Swenson Science Building. This artist has created three different ideas and I loved them all. One of the many gifts of our Chancellor is her commitment to the arts. Our campus has never looked better.

Art in public places is a wonderful advertisement for freedom. It says that we honor one person's interpretation of life and it makes us pause to see if we get it, like it, and will use it to fuel our own creativity. But art in public places carries a burden. If outdoors in Duluth, for example, the presentation must withstand winds of more than 50 miles per hour, temperatures from 30 below to 95 above, and retain its essential color in the sun (except for copper which is supposed to change). It must be large enough to have impact and usually four sided and three- dimensional. It must please us, provoke us, or stir us to new heights of awareness. And, finally, it must fit its surroundings even as it stands out.

I love coming across art in public places. It means we are brave enough to offer individual expression to an eclectic citizenry.

Can you imagine designing a 90 foot tall art piece for the out-of-doors in Duluth, Minnesota? You're an artist, Monette. What would you create?

September 4, 2003

"How to Stay Happily Married Should You Ever Marry"

1. Never marry for money, status or security. Marry for love.
2. Sing "I'm Forever Blowing Bubbles," "The Star Spangled Banner" or some such, together every night. Makes you happy.
3. Never hang wallpaper together. It is a justifiable cause for divorce.
4. Base your marriage on freedom and trust.
5. Play cards or Yahtzee or Scrabble three times a week.
6. Honor his family and never put them down.
7. Be loyal. Be faithful. Be cheerful. Be kind. Listen when he speaks.
8. When the going gets tough, go out for dinner and talk.
9. NEVER go to bed angry...no matter what.
10. If you marry an introvert, take care of him at a social event. He hates them.
11. As Nana always said, "Put on your makeup first thing in the morning."
12. Look as good at home as you would to see a friend for lunch.
13. Remember, spouses HATE to be nagged or scolded.
14. If you over-shop your budget, leave the evidence in the trunk until you feel good about it or until he is out of the house.
15. Never force a person to go to church with you. This is personal.
16. Make love every day.

September 5, 2003

"Three Things to Remember"

1. Always give someone her due.
2. Forgiveness means forgetting.
3. No one is all bad, or all good. We come in degrees.

"Cat Esme"

As you well know, Esme is in her teens and is a very smart cat, indeed. She is anti-social, totally independent, and devoted only to us. On weekends when we have cappuccino in bed, she sits between us waiting to lick the foam.

Whenever a visitor comes we say, "Don't pet the cat. She bites." Or as Max says, "She'll open up your vein." Twice a year someone doesn't believe us, and Esme attacks that person who is offering a hand saying, "I've never met a cat that doesn't like me." Esme is protective of those who feed her. She is the consummate tri-colored cat, just this side of wild. In the early years, when she would attack my ankle or hand, I tried squirting her with water from a squirt gun. It didn't stop her for a second.

Finally, I sat her down and said, "I love you just the way you are. We need to meet each other half way. I will stay out of your way until you want some attention." Things have been much better since our talk. I know all about her and she about me, and when I am down, there isn't a better friend.

Doctors Lucy and Mike, up the shore, are the only vets who know how to handle her. Even though they usually knock her out as she exits her cage door, they have understanding and compassion. In the past, I have had more than one vet tell me, "Never bring that cat back again. My staff will quit." So once a year, I bring Esme up the shore where she is sedated, probed and prodded, bathed and clipped, and given her shots. Upon returning home, she staggers out of the cage and literally drags her ample hindquarters to her bowl of food. Esme has always had a problem with obesity, but so far will not join Weight Watchers with me!

Remember when you and Mariko helped to pick her out in New Jersey? You two were attending Mt. Holyoke at the time and thought I should select the spunky female kitten and not the laid-back male. Sometimes I wonder...

September 7, 2003

"Keep Your Eyes on Me"

When I see children at airports and parents chasing after them, I am reminded how we solved this problem when you were little. Because you were very active and very bright and would not ride in a stroller or be hooked up to a leash, I told you that you could run anywhere you liked but you had to keep your eyes on me. And that you did. Every few steps away from me, you'd turn around and make eye contact, and yell, "I see you, Momma!"

Sometimes we forget how smart children are and how much they crave being trusted. You kept your eyes on me. And I was always there.

"Nana's Christmas Rice Pudding"

Here is Nana's recipe for her Christmas Rice Pudding. I try not to remember it is 10 points without the cream on the Weight Watchers chart. It was originally from Grandma Skomars, who was famous for her rice pudding. I am reading it from a recipe card in Nana's own writing and have gone over it with Patty. There is comfort in going through a disorganized cluster of recipes and coming across a loved one's handwriting. I have not tested it lately because it says to stir constantly for 1 1/2 hours. Let me know if you try it.

"Rub butter in the bottom and around a Dutch oven. Pour in 1/2 gallon of whole milk. Have it come to a boil gently. Then slowly pour in 1 FULL cup of rice (not instant) and about 2 teaspoons of salt and about 1/2 to 3/4 cup sugar. Stir often. When almost bubbling, turn down very low and simmer about 1 1/2 hours, stirring constantly. Stir in about 1 1/2 teaspoons vanilla."

Serve with cream, cinnamon, and an almond in one person's bowl to bring extra good luck in the coming year.

..

September 9, 2003

"Whomp the Yak"

Every time we go shopping, Max quotes Dave Barry, who once wrote a column about shopping called "Whomping the Yak." It seems that in the early years, men were sent out to kill a yak and bring it home to feed the family. Therefore, when a man goes to the mall, it is to pick up specific items like: socks, a Phillips screwdriver, and Listerine. He will return with just those items. Thus, he whomped the yak.

Most women, on the other hand, go to shop. They look at 80% of the items in the store, select a cart full of stuff, retrace their steps, returning most of it to the racks and shelves before checking out. This, according to Dave and Max, is **not** considered to be whomping the yak.

Of course what these gentlemen don't realize is that even though we completed our shopping list (plus added a bit more), we got home and tried on the new shoes with the new skirt only to realize they were two different shades of plum; although the new bedspread said "king size," they must have meant "queen size;" and we discovered the new cell phone we thought was on sale, was cheaper downtown. So we aren't done yet. We must return to the store to return the returns and turn around and shop some more.

So here is the lesson: be rested, have extra time, wear running shoes, carry bottled water and a power bar...enjoy the "hunting" and the discovery of designer jeans, 70% off, hanging in the wrong section, in just your size.

September 10, 2003

"Duluth Daughter"
There is not a nicer place on earth than Duluth on a September morn. With the tourists back home in Winnipeg and St. Paul and Chicago, and the kids back in school, I feel like I own my hometown. Take Canal Park. Most people start at the lighthouse and then go East taking the Lake Walk past the Viet Nam Memorial. I go the other way. And if I time it just right, I can turn around by the DECC (Duluth Entertainment Convention Center) and welcome another gigantic ore boat as it churns under the Aerial Bridge, and heads straight toward me, a Duluth Daughter. My heart skips a beat.

As Pops said, "Watch for the Orange and Black stripes on the stacks of the ore carriers. Pickands Mather Mining buys your shoes." Pops was a mechanical engineer. The last child of Jonas and Emma (Forsell) Skomars, E.T. Skomars was born January 13, 1909, at 40th Avenue West. Always a gentleman, smart, quiet in his ways and "nice looking." When they first met at an amphitheater, Nana said she thought he was a doctor.

Pops could take apart an engine, fix a little girl's bike and make a mean Denver sandwich for Sunday suppers. He would pull my loose teeth with his smelly pliers from the basement saying, "This is going to hurt me more than it is going to hurt you," which I never bought. He photographed me from birth until he handed me a camera and taught me how to use it.

Nana taught me to iron Pop's white shirts and handkerchiefs. It was an honor. Because he often came home with a surprise in his pocket for me (an eraser, pad of paper, stick of gum), I waited for Pop's arrival on the top step of the front stoop, or just inside the door in the cold months.

More than anyone else, Pops taught me to love Duluth. As his mother lay dying on the West side of town, I would drive with him from Lakeside to visit her. During those long drives (pre-free-way) he would tell me stories about the history of Duluth and the early years. Usually a man of few words, Pops would talk much more when he was behind the wheel. I always cherished my time alone with my Dad.

"One More 9/11"

Remembering 9/11 two years ago, this was a difficult day for me. Doesn't help that we have 95% humidity today.

I will never forget your calling me and being there for me. You suffered loss on 9/11 when your friends perished, but you took care of your mother.

May that day never be repeated.

"Your Frustrations"

Tonight you had a long list of frustrations. Someone hinted that the person you replaced in *The Laramie Project* might be returning. The birthday cake you baked for your friend, fell. Only Sheldon and Kathy from your family, are attending your opening.

What do you do with a bag of disappointments when it comes time for the curtain to rise? You have told me you simply "let it go." I would have trouble doing so.

When I carry a cluster of troubles with me, I find that the light goes out inside, I have trouble focusing on someone else, and I tend to wallow in "woe is me." So I like the fact that acting has taught you to put aside your list of worries as you go on with the show.

And as Nana used to say, "Trouble comes in threes." What we do with them is up to us. Thanks for the lesson.

September 13, 2003

"Opening Night"
You open tonight in *The Laramie Project*. How I wish I was there to see it. Savor this run of a script and story that can change the hearts and minds of those involved and those who bear witness.

This play will forever be a reminder that hate exists and crimes that follow do not go unpunished. In addition, Matthew Shepherd was so much more than his death, and his parents have spoken out about his life.

I thought about my friend Sharon whose son Aaron was a poet, addicted to drugs, a victim of abuse, and who took his own life. At Aaron's funeral, Sharon ended her remarks with:
"There were, therefore, many lights, as well as shadows, to his soul. I want the shadows and the lights of his life to be acknowledged and remembered here because they were both parts of loving him and of living with him. It is through the complex interplay of deep shadows with the many lights that I have learned so much more about how to be a human being.

It may seem to us now that these shadows claimed him, even as we reflect upon and share our fond memories of him. But maybe his death was his way to free himself from the shadows, the only way he saw as possible for him.

I want you to know that I love him, that I will always miss him. And, as I have told him before, he was the perfect son for me. This complex and beautiful son is the one I claim, and the one I now, with your help, must let go and say good-bye to, so that he can belong not just to me and to you, but to all of life."

Matthew and Aaron both died young for different reasons, by different means, but their mothers have been so very brave about facing their deaths and going on with life, somehow. I simply cannot imagine doing so.

"Buddhism"

The more I read about the philosophy of Buddhism, the more peaceful I become. I was born a Lutheran, literally grew up in the church, and will forever be a Lutheran, but I have taken additional journeys in order to cope with this crazy life. I am inspired by any non-violent philosophy (or person) that honors women, children, animals and whose leader does not possess great personal wealth. And also does not judge others or tell them what to think or do.

There are many paths to enlightenment, enrichment, and a peaceful heart. Meditation is a key.

It appears that except with intimates, one does not refer to being Buddhist. You just do it. You do not wear it on your sleeve insisting others follow but rather lead by example and meditate in private. It is a very lonely path; quite perfect for an introvert.

Tell me about your spiritual path, Monette. Please.

276   D I A N E   F A Y   S K O M A R S

September 15, 2003

"Home Depot"

If you ever feel blue, go to the parking lot of Home Depot and watch the customers go in and out for 30 minutes. Study them, really observe who they are or might be.

Today, while Max shopped, I watched the doors open and close at the exit sign. First out were a mother and daughter. The daughter carried two hanging plants, and the mom, in a wheel chair, followed with cans of paint on her lap. After placing her plants and the paint in the back seat, the daughter helped her mother into the van and folded up the wheel chair and deftly lifted it into the back. It was all quite matter-of-fact and probably well rehearsed over time.

Next came a guy, accompanied by a Home Depot clerk wheeling out a large three-sided shower unit standing upright in a cart. The figuring took a long time. Should the shower stall be placed open-end down or open-end up in the pickup truck, or should it stand tall? After much measuring and talking and joshing around, they decided to face it down in the bed of the truck. They each took a side and hoisted it for the journey ahead. Effortless. The clerk departed and the gentleman began the bungee cord wrapping, this way and that.

Then a grandfather and young grandson exited this hardware paradise. The grandfather appeared to be pre-occupied with the package he carried (I imagined serious tools) and paid no attention to the youngster. There was no package for the child. This was a man's trip! But as they were about to cross the parking lot, the boy reached up and took the free hand of his grandfather, who looked down and smiled.

And finally, a couple got out of their car next to me and left the car running with the a.c. cranked up for the two large dogs panting inside. Even if the environmentalists would have said to park a half block away in the shade and crank down the windows instead, for goodness sake, this was an act of kindness. The world is extraordinary in the ordinary, me thinks.

September 16, 2003

"Men"

This page is devoted to what I understand about men:

"Hey, Diana"

One of the things I love about Max is that he is not always the same guy. He invents other personas. Sometimes he is "Duke," the musician. Sometimes he is "Roy," a New Jersey truck driver.

When Max leaves town, "Roy" often calls:

"Hey, Diana! This is Roy. Is the magician in town? Wanna get together for some fun? I thought we could go bowling, ya know what I'm saying? Or just hang out."

All done in perfect New Jersey voice. This call makes me laugh even though I have heard it dozens and dozens of times.

I swear I married that guy for his humor.

"Packing Your Bag"

When I pack my suitcase, I start at my feet and work up my body. That way I rarely forget anything. Also I first pack twice as much as I need, and then take out half...kind of like shopping. Here is the list:

1. shoes, socks, boots
2. slacks, skirts, slips, underwear
3. tops, jackets, sweaters
4. belts, scarves
5. coat, jacket
6. hats
7. umbrella
8. jewelry, cosmetics, camera, book, cell phone, computer, clock, charge cords, dry breakfast cereal for snacks, glasses to match outfits, bags of wild rice as gifts, and thank-you cards to send on the way home

How do you pack your bag, Miss Monette?

"The Big Apple"
Rigorous day.
Up at 4:00 a.m. and on the road by 5:00
8:30 a.m. Meeting in the Twin Cities
11:30 a.m. Luncheon with UMD donors in St. Paul
3:00 p.m. Depart by plane for NYC
7:30 p.m. NYC arrival
I sure miss living in the Big Apple. It gave me energy and a million opportunities to explore the unknown. It also inspired me to practice small acts of kindness.

The Mayor told us to give only to charities and not to folks begging for change on the street. Yet there were some street people who just called to me. I set up some rules for myself. My limit was $5 a day. I never gave to people who used animals or children as props. I gave only to women. And I gave my bit of cash to those who were quiet about their message. It was difficult to pass by the others.

I was conned once by a guy who came out of a parking ramp saying he couldn't get his car out because his wallet was stolen. He was well dressed and well spoken. Would I please give him $20 to help him? I did, and later saw him doing the same routine at another ramp. When I approached him, he fled.

At the end of the day, anyone who has to stoop to begging or conning is in financial trouble. How can we not respond?

"His Holiness the Dalai Lama"

The scene was the Beacon Theatre on the West Side of NYC. My ticket was a gift from Lee and Donna. Most people in attendance were devotees of the Dalai Lama and dressed accordingly.

We sat near the front in this very full house. Monks were on the stage where there was a riser for His Holiness the Dalai Lama. When he arrived, some people bowed and lay down prone three times. I learned that His Holiness the Dalai Lama is a man with a message of peace and not a messiah of forgiveness. And yet, I felt like I was part of the whole of humanity because a light filled my heart and connected me to all others. The Dalai Lama has a radiance about him, an essence that cannot be denied.

Although he had a wonderful message of love, compassion and peace, it was his manner of warmth and gentle humor that touched me the most. (Had to discipline my eyes not to look at Richard Gere instead, who was next to His Holiness.)

Today held two gifts: being in the presence of the Dalai Lama and receiving the gift of the ticket from friends Lee and Donna. I am blessed.

September 21, 2003

"Central Park, Central Theme"
Another experience with the throngs who are here to bear witness and hear the words of the Dalai Lama.

He speaks globally and of peace. He believes each of us in our daily lives has opportunities to live in peace with each other. Individual acts that can multiply can have as much impact as those acts that come from people in powerful roles.

I have read that the Dalai Lama was born with his eyes open, which was one of several signs of whom he was to become. These two days have been amazing. I am determined to let this wave of inspiration wash over me every day of my life as I sometimes "swim" against high waves and other times float on tides coming into shore. I will also increase my meditation time.

Each act of kindness doubles the gesture and lifts your own spirit. Of that I know to be true.

DIANE FAY SKOMARS

"Man"

I read somewhere that the Dalai Lama, when asked what surprised him most about humanity, answered, "Man. Because he sacrifices his health in order to make money. Then he sacrifices money to recuperate his health. And then he is so anxious about the future that he does not enjoy the present; the result being that he does not live in the present or the future; he lives as if he is never going to die, then dies having never really lived."

How can we break this cycle of crazy?

September 23, 2003

"Work"

I have been thinking back to my career. Unlike you, who were "called to the theatre," I just sort of went where the door was open. Once I got into university/college life professionally, I stayed there for the most part.

It is funny because prior to working in higher education, one of the most rewarding years of my life was teaching third grade at a Roman Catholic School. I loved those third graders and the nuns who were full of life and didn't care a fig that I was Lutheran. At the time I was working at the phone company, and very unhappy about being paid to stop customers' service because they couldn't pay their bill. Responding to an ad in the newspaper, I contacted the school that needed a third grade teacher. I didn't teach religious classes, of course, but I did teach extra creative arts sessions. I remember we put on a play complete with costumes and music.

Every morning we went to Mass and then to class. I lacked the discipline to keep the peace, but most of the students were good as gold. My favorite student was Donde who once told me as she gazed out the window, "I can't do the math right now because I am thinking and dreaming." Made sense to me. She turned out to be a very smart and successful businesswoman and married into the Goldfine family, a family that I love.

DIANE FAY SKOMARS

"Your Name, Monette"

You would have been named "Donde" but for the fact that "Monette" came from the family. Aunt Fay suggested to my parents that I be named Monette. She had combined Pop's nickname (Monte) and Nana's name (Toinie) to create the name. When I was looking at Fay's photograph album and saw "Monette" written under *my* baby picture, I asked her about it. I liked it immediately.

When you were little, you didn't like your name. You wanted a name that was printed on pencils sold in the drug store. One year I got you pencils with your name on it. Special order for a special girl.

September 25, 2003

"The Grand Essentials"

Every night I read something from the Bible, from Buddhist teachings, and from a book, *The Promise of a New Day* by Karen Casey and Martha Vanceburg (Hazelton Foundation).

Tonight I read the following:

"The grand essentials to happiness in this life are

something to do,

something to love and

something to hope for."

By Joseph Addison

This sounds so simple...why do we make living life so hard?

"I Am the Sun"

When you were just four years old, Peter and I took you to Crookston, Minnesota, to visit the campus. Crookston is the home of the "sunflower." As you probably remember, sunflowers lift their pretty faces and follow the sun. I asked you to please stand among the flowers and lift *your* pretty face to the sun like the flowers. As I photographed you, I said, "Monette, you are my sunflower."

"No, Momma, I am the sun!" You always knew who you were.

September 27, 2003

"The Falling Leaves" by Jacques Prevert, Joseph Kosma and Johnny Mercer

Do you know this song? I used to play it on the piano and sing it to my heart's content when everyone was out of the house. It's beautiful, just like this time of year.

"The falling leaves drift by the window.
The autumn leaves of red and gold.
I see your lips, the summer kisses
The sun-burned hands I used to hold.
Since you went away the days grow long
And soon I'll hear old winter's song.
But I miss you most of all, my darling,
When autumn leaves start to fall."

This is a love song and describes perfectly how I feel about this time of year. Autumn is a time to remember past loves, the passing of summer, and the brilliant color nature provides for transition between seasons.

Soon the leaves, once a dazzling yellow, red and orange will drop to be crunched by feet and tires, and blown by a Northeaster into the woods where they will be covered by snow.

The songs I love make me cry, like this one. I will know I am dying when I no longer am moved by a melody with words from the heart. In the meantime I will sing to my hearts content remembering past autumns and past loves.

Please someday listen to the renditions of "The Autumn Leaves" by Eric Clapton and Edith Piaf, and Nat King Cole. My first choice will always be Nat King Cole's version.

"The Screen Play I Want to Write"

For years I have had this movie script in my head. I probably will never get around to writing it, but perhaps you can do it.

The setting is the North Shore of Lake Superior and the main characters are a sea captain (Finnish American) and his wife (Ojibwa). The crusty captain is close to retirement but looking forward to his next sail out of the Duluth Harbor on the longest ore boat on the Great Lakes. His wife is a practicing medicine woman and watches over her grandson when his momma works.

Their daughter (think a young Jessica Lange) is also on the boats and has made it through the ranks to just below captain. *Lake Superior Magazine* is doing a story about this father and daughter because both are sailing out of Duluth on the same vessel for the first time. Each is a bit wary of this arrangement because they have never worked side by side like this before and because their relationship is complicated. The father believes his daughter is too liberal, chooses bad male company for her young son, and that she should have become a school teacher instead.

The daughter thinks her father should have retired years ago because he drinks too much and it clouds his judgment. They love each other but they each have a fiery temperament and they are too much alike. You can see where this is headed.

Of course the story takes place in November on the great Lake Superior. This is the time of gales, but the real storm takes place aboard the ship. Under the scrutiny of a reporter and photographer, this father/daughter twosome hold it together for some time until the temperature drops, waves roll to unprecedented heights, and the wind roars combined with icy rain. Tempers flare about whether or not to take a safer but longer route, or a shorter route into the eye of the storm. Thus, the tale begins.

Please let me know if you want to work with me on this story of the human condition tested on the high seas. Maybe you could play the daughter.

September 29, 2003

"Donors Give so Much More Than Money"

Tonight I attended a dinner for scholarship students with their donor sponsors. This amazing couple opened their beautiful home high in the hills of Duluth and served dinner to thirty students. In addition these good donors told the story of their lives, business decisions and what motivated them to give back to UMD. Later the scholars shared their dreams for the future and thanked the donors for their gifts. I cannot tell you how much this evening meant to the students and to me. It is the reason I am in fund raising. **Giving back means getting back** and so much more.

"Management"

Today I was interviewed about my management style. It made me think about what it is. Guess it comes down to a few guidelines:

1. As a manager, I do not solve personality differences. "If you have a gripe with someone, go tell them, not me. If you cannot solve it after several meetings, come to me and I will settle the matter and neither of you will be happy."
2. If you have a major work problem to solve, come to me after you have considered seven solutions and selected three. Tell me those three solutions and which one you think is best and why you think so.
3. I no longer hire "high risk, high gain." It usually ends up to be high risk, period.
4. Delegate, delegate, delegate. Trust *and* check. Publicly recognize those that excel.
5. If an email message doesn't sit well, get up and talk to the person or at least call. Electronics can NEVER replace HUMAN contact.
6. Let no meeting end without each person at the table speaking their mind. The quiet person often has the solution because they have listened to everyone else.

When have you been asked to be a manager of people, and how did you manage it?

October 1, 2003

"WHITE RABBIT!!!" You got me.

****

"Kill the Surprise"

Today is a great day. For today is the birthday of pianist, Vladimir Horowitz, former President Jimmy Carter, and none other than Max Morath. Love that guy! He gets the cake.

Every year I try to give Max a surprise birthday party. And every year he thwarts them. I once reserved the Players Club in NY for a splendid brunch on his very day. I was going to ask Gene Jones to emcee; Bob Marks to produce it; Judy Carmichael, Reginald Robinson, Morten Gunnar Larsen, Butch Thompson and Bill Bolcom/Joan Morris to perform; his children to give toasts. But Max caught me xeroxing his Rolodex and he said, "No way!"

My therapist shared a story with me about a gentleman client who told his wife in no uncertain terms, "Do **not** plan a 75th surprise birthday party for me or I will divorce you." She did and he did. My counselor explained that her client's wife never asked him, "What would **you** like?"

So when I asked Max what **he** would like instead for his birthday, he said, "To take the *Queen Mary* to England and then fly on to Florence." Knowing when to cut my losses, I booked our trip and we had a fabulous time.

Lesson: surprise parties are often for the planner. (As you admonished me when I told you Max had squelched the party plans, "You just wanted to buy a new dress, Mother!") Best to ask the honoree what **he** desires.

"Frozen Assets"

There are a few lessons I have learned about money.

"Money is the root of all evil" is incorrect. As we learn in I Timothy 6:10 "For the *love* of money is the root of all evils," is correct. Money, by itself, is not what is evil but putting it first can corrupt.

Like most children you were very careful about spending your own earnings but remarkably generous with mine. I admired the parents that taught their children to divide their earnings in thirds: save, donate, spend. Did I try to teach you that? Probably not, because I have been a poor saver. We are both excellent spenders, however!

Pops taught me to pay off credit cards each month in order to never pay interest to those companies. When I failed to do so, I froze my credit cards in ice in the freezer. Remember the time you found my cards next to the ice cream and yelled, "Mother! Frozen credit cards? Really?" It now has become harder to just pay cash. Try it when you check into a hotel. They look at you like you have just robbed a bank.

I love it when I receive "found" money. It comes as a surprise...a refund, a check on my birthday, a twenty dollar bill forgotten in a pocket of jeans to be washed. I try to do something very special with it.

Lesson:

Money is funny, honey.

Control your spending, increase your lending, and save what's pending.

Think before you spend.

Cash is king. Checks are queens. Credit cards are jackals.

"Feedback"

This evening I spoke to your Sheldon. It was so good to connect with him. We spoke of you, of course, and your play. Sheldon said, "If I hadn't known the background, I would never have guessed Monette was new to the cast. She was that good!" He wished I had seen it. Me too. And it got me reflecting about reviewing your work.

Giving you feedback about your performances is difficult for this momma. I am never sure if I am to tell you the truth, be complimentary no-matter-what knowing the critics hammer all the arts, or just talk about the strengths of your performance. Your chosen field is fraught with pitfalls and I am so impressed when any of it works and that you have chosen this difficult path.

Years ago when you starred as Maria in *West Side Story,* I heard another mother tell her son what she thought he did poorly in the musical. I thought he would fall apart under such comments but, instead, he agreed with her and went on with what appeared to be an improved attitude and confidence. Their relationship was founded on the mother giving her honest opinion, good-bad-and-otherwise.

You and I buoy each other by talking about the strengths in the other. This seems to work for us. We must count on the other for support knowing the rest of the world will judge critically.

Years ago you told me, "Your job, mother, is to support me in the theatre no matter what, and I don't mean financially. Do not ask me what my backup plan is, whether I should get a master's degree in teaching, or if I should give up on acting. Just support me. This is my life."

Every mother wants smooth sailing for her child but it is the rough patches that build character. You are in a profession that gives you enough bumps in each production to last a lifetime.

What kind of feedback do you want from your mother?

"Dancing Memories"

After "dressing to the nines," we went to dinner and out dancing. How I love to dance! Am not sure I can get Max to dress up again soon, so will have to hold the night in memory a long while.

Max will never read these pages so I can tell you that Max proves that great musicians do not necessarily make great dancers. (Max says it is because musicians are always playing in the band.) I would think that this music man would make the right moves but he just does his own thing. We even took dancing lessons and he hated it. He didn't like to take direction. Most guys don't.

When I was a kid, I took dance lessons for years in Duluth. I just loved ballet and tap and I learned to move on the beat. In college I elected to take ballroom dancing and by then I was hooked. The freedom of the movement and the beautiful feeling of the body in motion are heightened by the fact that you are in unison with another.

Once I taught my brother to dance when he was going to the prom. He was nervous at first but turned out to be a natural at it. I remember I felt proud to be asked to help my big brother do anything. It was always the other way around.

Advice? Never ever turn down an opportunity to dance, my dear, and go ahead and lead if necessary.

October 5, 2003

"Our New Home"

I spent a few hours in our new home today. We move in three weeks and it sure feels good. Except for removing some wallpaper, there are no major changes. It is fate that we found it and Donde, my former student, was our real estate agent.

The owners left us a chair that matches the wallpaper, a table for the back porch, wine in the refrigerator and a map of the garden. Exceptionally good people. There was never a waver on either side or even one misunderstanding.

When we first walked in and had a look-around, Max and I met privately in the lower level and I said, "Write a check now. This is it." After three months of looking, you just know when it is right.

Advice? Write a check when it is the answer.

October 6, 2003

"Don't Smile Until Christmas"

When I taught third grade, a nun advised me not to smile until Christmas or I would have problems with discipline. I smiled and had problems the second day. How could I not smile until Christmas, I ask you? Loved the kids, the school, the Sisters, and the job. Just had to smile.

October 7, 2003

"Where Have I Lived?"

A new friend asked me to describe the dwellings I have lived in to date.

At the end of the list, he said he knew a lot about me. Here is my list:

House in Duluth, MN (twenty-eight years)
Rented house in Rockville, MD (less than one year)
Townhouse in Mendota Heights, St. Paul, MN (four years)
Townhouse in New Brighton, MN (two years)
"Eastcliff" University of Minnesota President's Residence (six years)
"Providence Point" University of Missouri President's Residence (two years)
House in Columbia, MO (six years)
Cottage up the North Shore of Lake Superior (four years)
House in Woodcliff Lake, NJ and an apartment in NYC (five years)
Back to the cottage up the North Shore of Lake Superior (one year)
House near University of Minnesota Duluth

October 8, 2003

"Where Have You Lived?"
Here is your list:

Mendota Heights townhouse in St. Paul, Minnesota (two years)
New Brighton townhouse in Minneapolis, Minnesota (two years)
"Eastcliff" University of Minnesota President's Residence, in St. Paul, Minnesota (six years)
"Providence Point," University of Missouri President's Residence in Columbia, Missouri (two years)
House in Columbia, Missouri (six years)
Mount Holyoke College residence hall (one year)
NYU residence hall and Chelsea apartment (three years)
Hollywood apartments
Pasadena perfect house
What can we conclude about you as we ponder your list of homes?

"Signs of the Times"

When I arrived on the campus of the University of Minnesota Twin Cities, I was working in Student Affairs. The campus, like most colleges and universities, was in turmoil over the Viet Nam War. In fact the student protesters sat down and closed down Washington Avenue, the main thoroughfare through campus. Eager to reclaim the street, the overzealous mayor of Minneapolis sent in helicopters with tear gas. I remember trying to get to Coffman Memorial Union by ducking in doorways to avoid the gas.

It was a tense time for my colleagues who tried to negotiate with the students. The administration hated the war also but recognized the dilemma of closing down a public road. The civil servant professionals in Student Affairs, many who were the ages of the graduate students camped out, were the go-betweens. They had to put aside their own strongly held opinions and serve the university. And the campus was a mess with posters, flyers and graffiti everywhere.

And here is why I tell you this story. In the midst of the tension and turmoil a science professor quietly began working on a plan to clean up the campus. He wasn't paid to do so, but he knew it was the right thing to do, and some made fun of him for trying. He began tearing down out-of-date posters, cajoling staff to clean up the graffiti, and lobbying the university to build kiosks for students to post information. He and Ed and I then worked on a campus policy about posters and the like. And I became the poster monitor until we could hire work-study students. I loved walking around campus and tearing down outdated material because it got me out-of-doors and I found out about the activities and programs of our 500 registered student organizations. After a few months the grounds began to look better and better and students had these neat places to really get their message out.

There were many heroes during these troubled times but one stands out, the science professor, who saw what needed to be done and had the courage to take it upon himself to change the environment.

"You Will Never See the Lace"

Remember the time you found out your boyfriend was involved with someone else?

You cried all night and slept with me. You took the morning off, had a bath and borrowed my credit card.

After buying all new lace underwear, you called him and said, "You will never see the lace!" And you never looked back.

"My Real Dilemma"

Of course the real dilemma in life is to ponder how I can be so fortunate to live at a time and in a country that has freedom, health care advantages, and no current civil war. On top of all that I have a great job, an exceptional daughter, a loving husband, a neat family, and a few close friends. And I travel. Who could ask for anything more?

But there is a rock in my shoe.

Shouldn't I be doing more to help the sick, the homeless, the hungry? Don't I realize that none of what I own is really mine even if I believe I earned it? And how dare I take a load of clothes to the Salvation Army only to shop for more? Does middle class always mean trying to climb higher and higher economically? And is writing a check ever enough?

Friends from the past lived in a designer home in the Twin Cities. When their kids left home for good, the couple sold their home and moved into a tiny bungalow and seemed blissfully happy. I asked them if they missed their beautiful house and their response was, "Heavens no. We enjoy our little nest with fewer chores. And now we get to give our money away and have the pleasure of making a difference."

Although I am in the business of fund raising for a university, I also must live with myself. When I am alone and I awake at night, I ponder why I am not doing more to help more.

Lesson: If you have the same dilemma, step up your giving of self and resources but leave the rock in your shoe as a reminder to do more.

"On Public Life"

Although I was never suited for public life, your Dad, Peter, was. He was the consummate public servant. He was a populist and as polite to those who called him at midnight as he was to those who met him by daylight. He treated his staff the same way he treated the rich and famous. And he worked tirelessly for the university.

Our public servants pay a terrific price for their positions. I have profound respect for Peter and for those who choose such a path.

I remember once when a disgruntled employee threatened to, "Shoot the President!" I drove up to Eastcliff and saw the University police stationed in the driveway. "Where is the President?" I asked. "Out jogging," was the answer. Peter was unfazed by such threats.

Another time when Peter was hung in effigy on campus, his mother, who was suffering from dementia at the time, pointed to her television and said with pride, "Look! It's my son Peter!"

Of course there are enormous advantages to living such a life. First and foremost are the exceptional people you meet. The Regents, politicians, the award-winning faculty, staff and alumni, distinguished guests of the university, donors, and the wonderful students. But there is a price to it all.

As an introvert, the public nature of living such a public life was extraordinarily difficult for me. I felt I was never really alone and yet I was lonely. I craved women friends and yet most of my previous friends working at the university had to distance them selves from me. ("I can't be seen with you because we are suing the university over pay for women, and Peter is on the list.") I loved serving the university but hated the way some would lobby me to get to the president. Marilyn and Jim were our closest friends and made our lives brighter.

I guess the lesson is to know yourself well before you sign on for life in the public arena.

October 13, 2003

"Go Toward the Roar"

Tonight our governor gave a stirring speech at the Chamber of Commerce dinner. He said that in Africa the female lions form a semi circle at one end and wait for the gazelles at the other end. When the gazelles arrive, a single, large, old tired male lion steps behind the gazelles and roars! The gazelles try to get away by fleeing away from this one old lion that roared, but they end up dying because the female lions are waiting.

His message is "go toward the roar."

I avoid noisy, blustery people who roar but maybe, just maybe, they are the harmless ones. I am rethinking my inclination. I am also wondering if the story is true.

October 14, 2003

"On Aging"

There is nothing so boring as a few words on "aging." However, as my daughter, you should know that turning 60 is a tough one for me. Not the age stigma, just the fact that I am in my final act (ages 60-90) and I feel it for the first time.

My energy level has changed. My searchfortherightword has increased. My aches have arrived. I won't even get into the wrinkles! No one ever says anymore, "You don't look a day over 45." The word retirement does not seem as remote.

The stimulation of my work keeps me going. I put in a tough day today. Up at 4 a.m., 3 airplanes, 3 hour drive to a donor dinner. So I guess I am still doing it, but I am aware for the first time, that there are limits.

DIANE FAY SKOMARS

"When You Need a Toast"

"Here's to the moment we've stolen.
'Though stealing is certainly wrong.
Listen to my sad, sad story,
Based on an old, old song.
If I had a barrel of apples,
and I left them out to rot,
And someone came by and stole them,
Would I blame her?
Certainly not!
For apples were meant to be eaten,
And moments were meant for delight.
And that's what we'll tell our conscience,
As we lie awake tonight."

With thanks to my mentor Edwin O. Siggelkow. An adapted version.

October 16, 2003

"About Being on Time"

The reason you are always on time is because you have Finnish blood. As Finns, we often arrive at our destination 10-15 minutes early and sit in the car to wait. Neighbors of the hosts find us suspect. We are never first to enter however; the second-to-arrive guests draw less attention to themselves.

Often we do a dry run before the event just to check out the address and circumstances. We hate surprises.

In New York City, everyone is late. "Couldn't get a taxi."

Same in L.A. except the reason is different. "The traffic was horrible."

This is understandable because few of them are Finns.

Lesson: to take the guesswork and anxiety out of attending an event or meeting at a new location, do figure out the destination ahead of time and arrive early and wait for the right moment to enter.

DIANE FAY SKOMARS

"You Got It"

You reached me by phone today at the airport and yelled, "I got it!" You will be in Arthur Miller's *All My Sons*. (And today is Arthur Miller's birthday.) Congratulations!

Your news will warm my heart all the day long. Even if I received the Nobel Peace Prize, I could not be happier. It is like that for a momma.

Happiness is reflected on many levels today and, perhaps, teaches us a few things.

1. Perseverance pays off.
2. Preparation pays off.
3. Passing it on pays off.

The first two are obvious. Number three is the most rewarding. When you have the glory, the honor and the part, reach out to another to help them achieve similar success. Networking is invaluable and works both ways. And your colleague will never forget your thoughtfulness and, in turn, can pass it on to another.

"Dressing for My Work"

Our alums are from all walks of life and have taken very different journeys. It is not enough to know about someone's career, family and apparent wealth. Rather it is important to consider their passion and the role the university played in their lives. Another clue to understanding an alumnus is to ask what their major *and* minor were in college. Often the major relates to future employment but the minor is their keen interest. That is why it is beneficial to meet the donors one-to-one, where they live.

Our visits today included a stop at a ranch for a barbeque. I advised Chancellor Martin that although they urged us to wear jeans, it usually means a fancy pair of jeans with a matching jean jacket and lots of bling. She wore a Brooks Brothers blazer and slacks and I went for the bling. I was wrong. They meant working jeans. So much for my wardrobe advice. We laughed.

I thought I knew the dress code for every major city and even the preferred colors. When I was the Alumnae Director for Stephens College, I learned that what you wear in South Florida (pastel jackets, sandals, straw hat), was not the same as Albuquerque (turquoise and orange with silver jewelry and boots) which sure didn't make it in San Francisco (suits, high end dresses, heels). The one thing I was always sure of was "wear black" in NYC!

Is there a dress code in L.A. besides skinny jeans, the highest heels, and tight tank tops?

Advice: before you visit, ask about the dress code and believe the advice.

"Professors"

We visited several donors today and it was very satisfying. We were there to thank them for their support, remind them of their ties to the university, and to have the Chancellor bring them up to date on UMD. It is fascinating to hear their memories of their time in Duluth: homecoming bonfires, amazing science experiments, meeting US senators and presidential candidates, picking up performers from the airport, meeting their intended under the arches of Old Main, being turned on to history for the first time, practice teaching, performing in a play, learning French, getting an internship in international marketing, and playing ice hockey.

Over and over our alumni tell us that it was a certain professor who made a difference in their lives. I believe we never forget the people who bet on us early, before we make our mark. UMD has always had an extraordinary number of outstanding teachers who reach out and encourage their students.

A professor who made an impact on me was one I never had for class. During the sixties and the anti-war movement, I had the privilege of talking to a science prof who had been a conscientious objector during WWII. It was not an easy path to take at the time. During the war, he was open to ridicule and the program was tough. My eyes were open to the idea that objecting *to* war could be life changing and powerful, and that although there was a price to pay, it was a recognized option.

What professor made a difference in your life besides the one who told you to leave Mount Holyoke and enter NYU and major in acting?

"Acknowledgements"

When someone does you a kindness, always offer thanks. In fact it is good to review kind gestures at the end of the day when there is still time to acknowledge them. A quick email message works or a call to their machine. And there is the hand-written note or postcard, more and more rare - therefore, all the more special.

If a friend sends you their poetry, short story, draft of a speech, photograph of their art piece, or a new DVD or CD, get right back to them with your feedback and thanks. It means a great deal.

I have also learned that everyone deserves a "well done" message when it is sincere. I have often called a person after a well-run meeting, major address or performance to say, "great job." I am equally impressed when a staff member plans an effective agenda, a creative room arrangement, or goes the extra mile to insure a successful event. Everything counts.

It takes so little and means so much when it is true. It is easy to believe that someone *knows* when they have done well, but it is not so. Everyone needs feedback.

Once I heard a very prominent person give a commence-ment address. I approached her to compliment her on her speech, and she hugged me and said, "Thank you so much. I wasn't sure I did a good job." She is a very accomplished woman so her response surprised me.

Who can you contact today to thank them or acknowledge their work?

"Stars"

"In one of the stars
I shall be living
In one of them
I shall be laughing
And so it will be
as if all of the stars
were laughing
when you look
at the sky at night."
The Little Prince
Antoine de Saint-Exupery

Have you ever been out in the countryside or desert and experienced the open sky at night? The stars can be dazzling and the constellations absolutely inspiring. If you are fortunate, you can forget yourself, your troubles and your woes, and allow the heavens to move you to a kind of weightlessness in which you are one with the atmosphere and space.

Never do I feel so small and yet so powerful. Never so helpless, but peaceful.

I wish for you, my star, many moments of weightlessness.

October 22, 2003

"When You Move"

Here is my advice when you move. "Don't."

But if you must, here is a list of hints.

Order flowers for yourself to arrive the afternoon of the move. Make sure you include a vase because you will not find yours until Christmas.

Use the occasion to throw out those items you hate, never use, or have enough of in your life. Have a box ready for Goodwill or the Women's Shelter. Prune your book collection. Some libraries will take them.

Always pack your own belongings. Moving company people will put a metal soap dish and a sponge in one large box with gobs of paper and barely protect the century old fruit bowl from your grandmother.

Get new, medium sized boxes, use newspaper for wrapping, and strapping tape on the outside, and mark each box on all sides with one of two codes: "A" means important; "B" means less important. And put the name of the room the box goes TO, not where it has come from. Again, on all sides.

Do not touch a box once packed or a piece of furniture. Hire for that. But do wear a lifting belt because you know you will lift something.

Hire strong people who are hungry for work to move you, and have a wad of twenties to give for tips and to anyone who helps. Have coffee, rolls and "Hello Dolly Bars" for everyone and if it is lunchtime, order pizza for all.

"When You Move" continued…

Before you move in, clean the place even though it has been cleaned. Put down new shelf paper in the kitchen because you will never do it again. Get all painting and wall papering done before the move.

Before the movers arrive, walk through the home with burning sage and chant, "Bless this house."

Pack your most precious items, cosmetics and health-related items in the car with you along with the cat in the cage.

Know ahead of time exactly where each piece of furniture will go. Be in the correct room when the movers come with your bureau, divan or table to direct them.

Get things done in this order: bed up and made; bathroom set; kitchen basics out.

Put the cat in a closet with her box, food and water, and place a note on the door: DO NOT OPEN!!! or you will never see her again. Cats adjust to a new dwelling in about a year.

Wear make-up, new jeans, cute shirt. Neighbors will be over to howdy you or peek through their window at you.

Order Chinese take-out the first night. Even if you sit on the floor, light a candle. It is a very special occasion.

(And when your friend is moving, always offer to pack boxes like our most generous friend, Maureen, did for us in Missouri. By the way, ask Maureen to tell you about her trip to Australia. You won't believe it could happen.)

What are your rules when you move?

"Leaving on a Jet Plane"

Of course it is not always easy to fly across the country, rent a car and drive to new places meeting people, often for the first time. There can be delays, rain or sleet or hail, mix-ups in arrangements, bad hotels, detours and lost luggage. Did I ever tell you about the time I lost my bag and it travelled the world for one year only to arrive at my door with half my belongings and that of a man who favored 2x Hawaiian shirts?

For all the traveling I have done in my life, I still over pack. My suitcase is usually the largest and the heaviest. My carry-on is not a suitcase but rather a very large, open-at-the-top, canvas bag that holds my essentials. I put it at my feet and use it as a footrest. I have a favorite book, slipper socks, windbreaker, food and water. Except to greet another, I generally don't speak unless spoken to and shudder when the person behind me insists on using a big voice to describe her life, endlessly, to her seatmate.

I am always amazed when I fly that all of it works as well as it does. Millions of people get on airplanes daily, land at their desired destination, and leave the terminal with their own luggage. For the best passengers, there appears to be a kind of unspoken airplane etiquette:

1. Don't push on the seat ahead of you.
2. Ask permission before you tip your seat back.
3. Speak in a quiet voice at all times.
4. Keep your dog in the carrier.
5. Use sugar in any form to quiet a child.
6. Be pleasant to the steward and pass on your magazines.
7. Do not ask to visit the pilot.
8. Cover up "R" rated movies from children on your dvd player.
9. It's okay to sleep as long as you don't drool and snore.

10. Be cool if they're overbooked and you are bumped up to first class and seated next to Peter Fonda. Pretend *you* are the star and he is a retired schoolteacher.

11. And if you believe this list, you are as loopy as your mother.

October 25, 2003

"Slipping Through My Fingers" (from *Mamma Mia, by ABBA)*

"School bag in hand
She leaves home
in the early morning
Waving goodbye with an
absent-minded smile
I watch her go with a surge
of that well-known sadness
And I have to sit down
for a while
The feeling that I'm
losing her forever
And without really
entering her world
I'm glad whenever
I can share her laughter
That funny little girl
Slipping through my fingers
all the time
I try to capture every
minute
The feeling in it
Slipping through my fingers
all the time
Do I really see what's
in her mind
Each time I think
I'm close to knowing
She keeps on growing
Slipping through my fingers

all the time
Sleep in our eyes
Her and me at the
breakfast table

"Slipping Through My Fingers" continued...

Barely awake,
I let precious time go by
Then when she's gone
There's that odd
melancholy feeling
And a sense of guilt
I can't deny
What happened to those
wonderful adventures
The places I had planned
for us to go
Well, some of that we did
but most we didn't
And why I just don't know
Slipping through my fingers
all the time...
Sometimes I wish that
I could freeze the picture
And save it from the
funny tricks of time
Slipping through my fingers
Schoolbag in hand
She leaves home
in the early morning
Waving goodbye with an
absent-minded smile"

This song from *Mamma Mia* always brings tears. (music and lyrics by ABBA)

October 27, 2003

"In Your Own Words"

I love what you have written on your web site: www. monettemagrath.com about your life:

"Monette was born in Minneapolis, MN. Growing up, her parents often took her to the Guthrie Theatre, Northrop Auditorium and the Children's Theatre Company. At home, she had her own puppet theater where dinner guests were invited to see a variety of original shows. At around the age of seven, she would frequently perform the dying swan from *Swan Lake* in the living room - in a purple tutu. In elementary school, she played an ant in *The Ant and the Grasshopper* - important because it was her first speaking role: "We have work to do." Her grandmother claimed that Monette said she wanted to be an actress when she was three. Monette does not remember saying or thinking this, all evidence to the contrary..."

The only thing I would change is that you were but four years old when you were a swan dying in the living room. I remember that you were very serious about the scene. There were no giggles, no embarrassment, no self-conscious comments. You held your composure and your audience. You set the stage for your life to come.

"You In Tutu"

DIANE FAY SKOMARS

October 29, 2003

"I'm Looking Over a Four Leaf Clover"

When I was four years old, I sang this song on the local radio station. It was recorded on a disc that I still have. Here are the words of the chorus:

"I'm looking over a four leaf clover that I overlooked before;
One leaf is sunshine, the second is rain,
Third is the roses that grow in the lane,
No need explaining, the one remaining
Is somebody I adore.
I'm looking over a four leaf clover that
I overlooked before."
(Lyric by Mort Dixon and Music by Harry Woods)

The reason this song comes to mind is a memory about Nana. She could step into a yard or a field, and walk right up to a four leaf clover. She placed them in her shoes. She sang this song to me and told me she believed that the four leaf clover brought her good luck all her life.

I am wondering if you can easily find four leaf clovers. Maybe they don't grow in L.A. If not four leaf clovers, what object do you believe brings you good luck?

"Stuck Sucks"

When you feel you are stuck, change your perspective:

1. Write down your situation, turn the paper upside down and study it.
2. Look at the palm of your hand, fingers open. Study the spaces in between your fingers and consider *them* the reality, the positive, the shape to regard.
3. Create a continuum from taking no action, to taking some action, to going all out. Decide your next step.
4. Walk two vigorous miles out-of-doors.
5. Consider seven solutions.
6. Call a person you admired long ago and ask them how they are.
7. Watch for a sign in a new direction.
8. Chant "Let go, let God" one hundred times with palms upward.
9. Bake "Hello Dolly Bars" and bring them to a neighbor.
10. Try a new perfume.

"HAPPY HALLOWEEN"

We were busy tonight giving out candy to the kids in our new neighborhood. Esme decided to go as a cat this year.

While I was growing up, Halloween was celebrated going door-to-door with a pillow case for collecting the loot: pennies, homemade popcorn balls, candy (wrapped and unwrapped), apples, peanuts, bubblegum, homemade fudge wrapped in wax paper, taffy, cookies, and once an I.O.U. from Mrs. Anderson who was out of treats. It generally snowed and in spite of wearing my winter jacket, my costume from dance class would be soggy and drooping by the end of the evening.

Once home I would spread the goods out on my bed and count the money while eating the fudge, put the apples in the kitchen, give the dog the cookies, and divide the multiples into piles. My brothers would want to trade with me but I would hang on to the gum, nutty peanut butter chews in black and orange wrappers, and anything dark chocolate. They knew which houses gave out dollar bills and full-size Hershey chocolate bars! My half-full pillowcase would then go under my bed to be visited over the next week or two after school, until the good choices were consumed. And then it was forgotten until about Easter week when we did Spring house cleaning and discovered dog, Heather, had chewed on the rest.

The few children that are now allowed to go door-to-door miss out on the homemade fudge, cookies and popcorn balls. No trust. Parents hover in the background and hurry the children away if you ask about their costumes.

You, Mosie, loved Halloween because you could dress up! You were never as interested in the candy as you were in your costume.

November 1, 2003

"WHITE RABBIT" I got you!

****

"Diane Meets Diane"

Did I ever tell you how I met my friend Diane? We were living in New Jersey and I had left behind my friends, my job and my home in Minnesota. Max was on the road a good deal and I was casting about to find my purpose. It was a very lonely time for me initially.

One day I was driving to the grocery store and I said out loud, "God, please send me a friend!" Around the next corner was a woman in a motorized wheel chair, stopped in the middle of the road. Cars were driving around her! I pulled over and went to her and before I could speak, she asked, "What is your name?" "Diane," I said. "Then God has sent you," she replied.

Her chair was out of charge and was pretty hard to push, but we got to the curb and I found out she lived in an apartment about a block and a half away through a field. Off we went with me huffing and puffing, and Diane telling me her life story. Diane was the victim of a head injury from a bullet in her youth and was partially paralyzed. Often she would get in her battery-operated wheel chair and go to the store, but on that day, her chair quit on her. Thus began our friendship.

After learning to handle her unmotorized wheel chair and getting her into the car, we were off and running to shop, have lunch out, go to the park for a picnic, and take road trips to visit her lovely mother. Diane and I laughed, we cried, we railed about politics. We became friends. Recently she reminded me that I walked in her honor at the Million Mom March in Washington D.C., 2000.

You might think this was a one-way relationship with my giving her rides and shopping trips but I assure you I received far more than I gave. Diane is a smart, fun-loving, positive woman who has made peace with her situation and has served on statewide organizations to help people like herself. Although we write to each other from time to time, I still miss her, and I am the godmother to her cat, Precious. I wish for you such a friend.

November 2, 2003

"What You Don't Know About Me"

1. Years ago I wrote an advice column for a newspaper.
2. In response to my first request for a kiss by a boy named "Tommy" I asked, "Will my hand do?" (sixth grade)
3. I set my watch fifteen minutes ahead. Always have. Always will.
4. Once I wrote several tales of intrigue.
5. I have always been led by signs.
6. I have loved six men and many more women. (Definition: I would take a bullet for them.)
7. I once piloted a plane over Lake Superior.
8. While in college, we started a service sorority.
9. I have "met" four United States Presidents. (Presidents Clinton, Bush, Carter, Kennedy)
10. I once tried to smoke marijuana in Jamaica but it didn't work for me.
11. I have never viewed my adult years alone as "between marriages," but rather, as being solidly single.
12. I have visited over sixty countries.
13. In college I had a jazz program on the KUMD radio station. It is possible that Pops and my academic advisor were my only fans.
14. I once dreamed of becoming a Lutheran minister but women weren't allowed. I was, however, an active member of the Duluth Women's Liberation Movement in the late sixties, early seventies.

DIANE FAY SKOMARS

"We've Got Troubles"

As I was unpacking, I came across the wedding announcement for Peter's and my wedding in 1978. You were just four years old and, of course, stole the show. Your favorite teddy bear had lost an eye and so we put a sprig of baby's breath in the socket until we could bring it to the "hospital." You were darling about it.

Before the wedding, there were sirens and I told you, "Someone's got troubles." As the fire truck stopped outside of our new home, "Eastcliff," you turned to me and said, "*We've* got troubles." A fire in the furnace room was quickly extinguished and the wedding went on without a hitch, so to speak.

What do you remember about that day?

November 4, 2003

"Bag It at the Door."

You open this week in *All My Sons*. It sounds like another powerful play. Know you will "knock 'em dead."

I truly don't know how you do it. Night after night playing someone else, a someone with lots of sorrow. I can hardly play myself each day much less another.

Your daily preparation for your role fascinates me. You do voice exercises up and down the scale at intervals of a third. Your mirror in the Dressing Room has beautiful photographs and pictures depicting the era and place of the production and you study them. You listen to timely music. And your hair, makeup and nails are spot-on for the part you play. Minute by minute you transform yourself into a scientist, lover, socialite, mother, comedian, or tortured soul.

At the end of the performance do you un-do all that you did to prepare for *All My Sons*, in order not to arrive home as "someone with lots of sorrow?" In other words, does the character you play linger in you in real life? Or can you cast it all off as just another gig?

In my life I try to shed my university work at the door of my home but it is hard to do so. I am the person who had to make tough decisions, or who made a mistake, or who is worried about preparation for tomorrow's 7 a.m. meeting, who walks in the door. It takes an hour or so to unwind. Et tu?

Lesson: Bag it at the door or at least tread softly upon re-entry. The other person in your life has been functioning in real time, in real life.

November 5, 2003

"Chicago to the Max"
Today I found out that Max had a TIA (mini stroke) and my world seemed to stop...
With the help of Kit, Lucy and Maryann, I did what I had to do.
I drove to Chicago where he was to perform and HOORAH! He's okay.
Thank you, God!
Monette, when potential crisis hits, drop whatever you're doing and go to that person in trouble. Knowing who and what are most important in your life is critical.

"A Crooked Family Tree"

Last week I ran into a former classmate who told me he had been happily married for years "just once to the same woman." I congratulated him as I always do when I hear about a strong, long-term marriage, and then he went on to say, "It must be hard to have been a failure at marriage."

I told him that if he was talking about *my life,* I didn't focus only on failure but viewed my life in chapters. I believe that it is not only about the length of time one remains in a marriage but the quality of that marriage. I then explained that I have met some couples that have long-term but "dead" marriages, and that I don't admire them any more than I do divorced folks. Of course no one wants a divorce because **everyone** suffers, and it is extremely painful for the couple and the family. But with the divorce rate over 40%, it seems like an important subject to study.

Felt kind of shaky for speaking up in this way but I get weary of people who ask, "How many times have you been married?" "Who is your daughter's real father?" "What was your last name in the seventies?" It seems rather rude.

I would really prefer to talk about important matters like war, politics, women's issues, and books I am reading.

You, my dear, have somehow made a crooked family tree stand proud and tall by honoring each of us and staying in close communication. I salute you.

"Women Friends"

Nana taught me the importance of having women friends. Some of my earliest memories are of Nana having women over for coffee or going to their homes for a "cuppa" (coffee). I cannot remember their exact conversations but I do remember their covering the latest world news, the lives of neighbors, the church and the P.T.A. (Parent Teacher Association) doings. They always wore dresses and there was lots of laughter.

These women were kind of a support group. They shared some laughs, their ups and downs, hot dish recipes, cures for ailments, and proudly showed each other the afghan or quilt they were working on. At some point a couple of them took up painting statuary and our house began to fill with figurines and even hand-painted lamps.

No one ever just dropped in. These coffee sessions were planned in advance by telephone. In those days, there was one phone in the entranceway of our house and we had a party line that meant others could listen. Our telephone number was 525-1191. It must seem quaint.

Nana often reminisced about her girlfriends before she was married. She said they sometimes dressed alike in sailor outfits and took trips to area lakes and the boys would follow them. She described them as carefree times and said she had a ball.

I believe that women friends are there at the beginning of your life and at the end and, if you are fortunate, in between.

Who are your closest girlfriends, and when you meet for a "cuppa" (now at Starbuck's), do you share your ups and downs and is there laughter?

November 8, 2003

"Nana and Her Girlfriends in 1930"
 She's on the left.

DIANE FAY SKOMARS

November 9, 2003

"Mr. Ragtime"

As I wrote earlier, Max Morath has performed five thousand shows in 60 plus years. He cancelled only three times. Once for an operation, once for a TIA, and once for his grandson Eric's bar mitzvah. His stories about the road are the stuff of legends: he played by flashlight when the electricity went out at a seminary in rural Louisiana; a June bug flew into his mouth while singing "The Eyes of Texas" at an outdoor event near San Antonio; in San Francisco, Max's agent watched a bankrupt club owner count the money, and the agent took what was owed Max in a paper bag and ran out the back door to the waiting van; and his favorite stage jacket (plaid!) was made from upholstery material, 100 % polyester, "so it would never wrinkle."

Max was invited to the White House when President Lyndon Johnson signed the public television bill in 1967. Max has performed for the rich and with the famous. He has mentored countless young musicians and lectured on ragtime, popular music, and "Technology and the Performing Arts." He has composed beautiful rags and songs but also created jingles for AT&T, Beechnut Peppermint Gum and Kent Cigarettes. He has written articles, chapters and entire books. And he makes a mean Greek omelet.

He has earned his place in ragtime history and in my heart, my Maxie.

November 10, 2003

"Get Back on the Horse"

I quoted you today. Max asked if he should play his show next week, following his Chicago health scare. He decided to follow your advice and "get back on the horse."

You always did and I hope you always will.

DIANE FAY SKOMARS

"A Good Day"

Today I worked with a generous gentleman to create a new scholarship; heard back from a stellar couple that have agreed to head up a UMD fund-raising campaign; listened to a woman who wants to remember her son, who died at a young age, with a gift to the university. This is such rewarding work. I am often moved to tears. God bless the donors.

My advice for you is to choose a career path that brings you joy and satisfaction, and to realize there may not be just one path. Each job can bring different satisfaction. Never stay stuck in one field only. Keep all your options open and try new opportunities in order to grow. (I know you do not want to hear this because acting "is the only thing I love to do.")

Once, when I couldn't decide about leaving a position, a friend said to me, "Are you waiting for a gold watch for 25 years of service? Diane, it is NOT about how long you stay, but rather what you accomplish while you're there."

November 12, 2003

"It's Beginning to Feel a Lot Like Home"

Tonight for the first time we sat in the living room at dusk and it felt like home. We have been unpacking and unpacking, and the house began to represent WORK only. So it felt good to just sit.

I was reminded why I like this house. The three birch trees out the front window recall my Minnesota roots and the beauty of the earth. The setting sun through the picture window creates a warm glow in the room, and the sounds of the house reacting to the autumn winds are friendly. We built a fire in the fireplace and sat with tiny glasses of Finlandia Vodka, hardtack, pickled herring, and Havarti cheese, all in celebration of a house well chosen and our good fortune.

Esme is still trying to figure out the house and is seen wandering room to room hunting for mice and ghosts. No sightings yet.

Lesson: don't compromise on the purchase of a house. It's worth the wait.

November 13, 2003

"Viet Nam, Thailand, Cambodia"

The package I have been waiting for arrived from the film processors in NY. It contained my photographic enlargements of Viet Nam, Thailand and Cambodia from the amazing trip I was on with my good friend Donna and other women, and expertly led by friend Jean of "B.J. Adventures." Next I plan to turn the photographs in for framing. It felt so good! Actually, I was amazed by them. Did I really take those photographs?

My shrink has me listing my accomplishments and it is a tough assignment. Photography is one I feel good about, however.

What accomplishment do you feel best about, Monette?

"Not Bad"

I have a doctor friend who is about 70 years old and by Hollywood standards, less than handsome. He told me that every Monday morning he takes a shower, dries off, and stands in front of a full length mirror, buck naked, and says, "Not bad, Justin." He then takes a side view, back, and other side, and each time he says, "Not bad, Justin." Isn't that a great way to start the week? I could do it as long as I take off my glasses.

Remember to own your body as yourself and give yourself credit, buck naked and otherwise.

November 15, 2003

"Christmas Gifts"
  Today I worked on Christmas gifts. Here is my list this year:

1. Max - leather desk set and framed oil portrait of himself
2. Buzz - handmade Cosanti wind chimes from Scottsdale
3. Warner - UMD jacket for this alumnus
4. Judy - Gift Certificate for Cold Water Creek and a Swarovski piece
5. Patty - fuzzy slippers and a copy of my favorite book
6. Christy - Viet Nam place mats and homemade scarf
7. Kathy - Indigo silk shirt and handmade purse
8. Bob - shirt to match his eyes
9. Paula - p.j.'s and purse with a Hawaiian theme
10. Malia - clothes and Dream Catcher made by a Native friend
11. Fred - wallet, Mets t-shirt and Indian incense
12. Jordan Claire - turtle necklace from Thailand and teddy bear
13. Michael - a book for this ace golfer
14. Eric - leather journal, globe
15. David - ring and leather journal
16. Amy - book on cats
17. Fay - favorite hand cream
18. Denise - leather cap from Italy
19. Effie - Finnish notepaper
20. Roy - framed photograph of us in 1949 coming out of the ocean
21. Scott - Viking calendar
22. Diana - special box
23. Dan - firehouse recipe book
24. Donna - Thailand jewelry
25. Family in Finland - in process
26. Gals at work - in process

27. Sheldon's parents - Harry and David's "Tower of Treats"
28. Frances - flower stationery
29. Girlfriends - scarves from Viet Nam
30. Monette and Sheldon - aren't you curious?

It's a good thing I shopped all year.

DIANE FAY SKOMARS

"Fog"

Today's fog was dense and damp. To quote a famous author, "A good day for a murder." Was glad for the gloom because I had to clean the house from top to bottom, and knew I wasn't missing much out-of-doors. I am deeply affected by the weather.

It isn't so much the temperatures that can get me down living up North, but rather, the lack of sun. November, March and April can be deadly to say nothing of October and May. My friend uses a sun lamp to pep up and many flee to the South in the dreary months. I travel for my work so I miss some of the worst of times. I notice, however, that when the sun is out, it inspires, brings smiles and hope, adds spring to our steps, and a kind of joy to our hearts.

I bet the reason the film industry settled in Los Angeles was to keep the actors ever hopeful for a job and the cameras always ready for another shoot out-of-doors.

Enjoy your California sun-drenched days, but never forget you were born in the North where no one takes a sunny day for granted.

November 17, 2003

"Future"

I have now worked for one year and one month at the university, this time. Of course this is my third time working here. I had planned to stay until age 62 but the Social Security benefits were changed to age 63 so I must work for a total of four more years or more, probably much more.

Rarely in all my life have I thought about or planned for my retirement. I have no concept of it. Work has been a dominant factor and I always figured I would continue to work at something and just keel over. It's funny because in development we often talk to donors about their wills, their retirement, their future plans. I guess this is a case of the dentist having a mouth full of cavities.

Perhaps I should admit that ending a career could be a wonderful opportunity to reinvent myself and create a good future. In the mean time I will continue to concentrate on my job but spend a bit more time dreaming in the realm of possibilities.

Monette: it is a good idea to keep your options open, commit to the present, but do a bit of planning for the future. Although this clearly isn't my strength, it could be yours.

DIANE FAY SKOMARS

"When the Music Changes, so Does the Dance" African Quotation
    Wise people tell you to take charge of your life and make it happen.
    Other wise people tell you to go with the flow.
    Both are correct.
    There are times, my dear, when moving on is the right thing to do. It should come, however, after you have examined the situation from every side and made **major attempts** to change things and let a great deal of time go by. However, if there is a brick wall in front of you that will not come down, and you cannot fly over it, dig under it, or go around it, move on.
    Other times, you will experience easier times when the planets seem to be aligned and when the universe appears to be in your favor. That is when you can let go and let the natural forces advise you.
    I love the African quotation above. Indeed life does call for a new dance when that music changes. Have you experienced this in your good life?

"Christmas 2003"

This Christmas will be a big change because you and I will not be together. It changes our tradition. But I respect the fact you don't feel I should come without Max. I am not sure why you feel that way since we don't mind if I come alone, but I accept it.

Max is funny about Christmas. He says he has done enough of them. Although he is generous about my gift buying, he is Scrooge-like about the holidays.

Years ago I listened to a speaker who urged us to experience Christmas in a land that does not speak English. He said we are trapped into trying to duplicate the perfect Christmas from our youth each year. Believing it is not possible, he said to break away from everything and everyone and try on a new culture. Perhaps this is the year to try it. As always, I will search and find Baby Jesus in person or in action. My personal Christmas touchstone.

Friend Maureen told me about the time she went to a Spanish speaking Christmas mass and the congregation jangled their car keys to the rhythm of "Silent Night." She said she will never forget the sound.

Although it is difficult to think of Christmas without my girl, I understand and will move forward. Also, the two of you can relax and enjoy each other and not have to worry about company. Thank you for being honest.

"Pops and Nana on Their Wedding Day"

"Beaujolais Nouveau"

Each year, just before Thanksgiving, our university black tie dinner is held at the Glensheen Estate. Our donors are thanked for their many gifts to the university and there is a well-deserved tribute to our Chancellor. With Thanksgiving just around the corner, it is the perfect time to give thanks. And I never forget that the Congdon family itself gave the university the mansion when the last family member died. The unveiling of the new wine, with all its promise, adds to the celebration.

Your Grandfather, Pops, had a special connection to Glensheen. During the depression, he was a chauffeur for the d'Autremont family and was in charge of driving Mrs. d'Autremont to tea with Mrs. Congdon at Glensheen. He said he waited in the kitchen with the staff and he wore a uniform. Through Pops, I grew up hearing stories about this beautiful estate and the family. Therefore, when the university was given the gift of Glensheen, it was easy to advise, "Do not sell it!" Now everyone can enjoy it by attending special events and participating in tours.

Do you remember when we visited Glensheen shortly after it was given to the university? Some of the areas were cordoned off by yellow police tape. You were a little girl and fascinated by the beauty of the mansion and totally unaware of the recent tragedy that had taken place in the house. Although it is easy for adults to be focused on the Glensheen murders, the other story is the generosity of the family.

November 22, 2003

"The President's Spouse"

At the Beaujolais Nouveau dinner, I was told that 65 university president spouses now have contracts with their institutions to recognize their role and their jobs in support of the president and university. Perhaps the work we did long ago on the book, *The President's Spouse: Volunteer or Volunteered?*, has helped others. I hope so.

I hope you still have a copy of that book, Monette. It was an attempt to understand and to explain what it is like to be in partnership with a public, educational figure. It was told by married partners across the country and based on a survey, thanks to Roger and Joan. There is a price to "going public" with your spouse. The loss of privacy, the sheer demands of the role, the necessity of living in a university-owned home, and the expectations, can be quite overwhelming. And, of course, there are the children and how their lives are affected.

What price did you as a child pay for living in the University of Minnesota's "Eastcliff" and the University of Missouri's "Providence Point?"

November 23, 2003

"JFK"

Forty years ago today President Kennedy was shot in Dallas. Like 9/11, everyone can tell you where they were when they heard the news from Texas. I was a student at UMD at the time and we all gathered around a radio speaker in the student center and were horrified by the news. Nana and I spent the weekend glued to the television set with both of us crying. As a Republican, Pops refused to watch, and we were furious at him. It was only one of three times I was disappointed in my father.

President Kennedy spoke at UMD just a short time before his death. There was a rumor later that Lee Harvey Oswald was possibly in the Duluth area when the President was here. I doubt that it was true.

"Ask not what your country can do for you, but what you can do for your country," was the President's most famous quotation.

What were you taught in school about this tragedy? And what might you do for your country?

November 24, 2003

"Love Actually"

Run, don't walk, to this film! It is a story about love and begins with scenes at an airport where people are greeting each other with hugs and kisses. It shows the universality of the human touch, and that love is all around, if only a person would open her eyes and see the obvious. It is also a bit naughty.

Where do you see love?

"Anxious"

I am getting anxious about giving you this journal. I wonder what you'll think. Too corny, too presumptuous, too quirky? Gulp! Dare I give it to you?

I hope you will put it away for a rainy day in 2033. What will the world be like for **you** 30 years hence? Hope your life will be filled with love and the "lightness of being." If not that, I hope it is messy and filled with intrigue and involvement. Either way, your essence is "goodness" and that won't change.

November 26, 2003

"SISU"

You have heard this word all your life, my dear. It is the word that helps define your Finnish heritage. All four of my grandparents came from Finland. As you know, Finland was part of Sweden for centuries and the Skomars name is actually Swedish. Because Pops had little interest in his family tree going back, I didn't have the strong ties that existed on Nana's side.

Nana's Finnish family names were Niemi and Kuusisto. Since Nana's father's name was changed to Johnson when he reached this country, I always wondered if his Kuusisto family cared about his new name. On one of our visits to Finland I asked Grandpa Johnson's brother if the name change mattered to his family. "Not at all. We were glad John was able to go to America."

As for the word *sisu*, it simply means "guts or courage." And your family-of-old had it. It takes *sisu* to:

*come to America and leave your family behind never to see them again;

*clear the land and farm in northern Minnesota and help form the local cooperative movement (Grandpa John W. (Kuusisto) Johnson);

*raise a large family, create gardens that fed the family and farm hands, become a trusted mid-wife, write poetry (Grandma Hilja (Niemi) Johnson);

*live in Duluth and become a house moving contractor after being shot in the Spanish American War (Grandpa Jonas Gabriel Skomars);

*raise a large family, lose your husband when your youngest is 15, and run a cottage rental business on Lake Superior (Grandma Emma Christina(Forsell) Skomars)

Your goal to create an acting career in Los Angeles takes enormous *sisu*. I just wanted you to always remember you come by it naturally, and you have broken new ground.

November 27, 2003

"Happy Thanksgiving"

My happiest memories of Thanksgiving come from our time in Columbia, Missouri. You and I had a turkey in the oven all day, the sun was pouring in, and it was warm enough to spend time on the deck with our pets, dogs Molly and Bandit, and Mouse the cat. Besides the turkey, you loved the candied sweet potatoes and put up with my tamale dressing (my favorite). We had tons of food that lasted all week, occasional guests, and we would watch our favorite movies.

Remember the time I forgot to thaw the huge turkey, and I put it in the tub to unfreeze? We came home to find the pets watching it float around the bathtub with Bandit barking all the while. With only one leg, Mouse couldn't really attack it, but Molly tried. Never mind. We ate it and it was delicious.

DIANE FAY SKOMARS

November 28, 2003

"Tamale Stuffing for the Turkey" (with thanks to my friend, Pud, for the inspiration)

Two cans of meat tamales, get rid of the paper wrappers but save the sauce

Onions and celery cooked in butter until translucent

Bag of Pepperidge Farm stuffing, follow the directions (butter and water)

Break up the tamales and mix ALL ingredients together. Bake separately.

I know you don't approve of this recipe, youCalifornia-healthygreengirl, but some day you will thank me for adding ZING to your Thanksgiving dinner.

Reminder: because it is not safe, never stuff the turkey. This advice is from Chef Matt.

"Jack London" (a favorite quotation by London, from Neale)
"I would rather be ashes than dust!

> I would rather that my spark should burn out in a
> brilliant blaze than it should be stifled by dryrot.
> I would rather be a superb meteor,
> every atom of me in magnificent glow,
> than a sleepy and permanent planet.
> The proper function of man is to live,
> not to exist.
> I shall not waste my days
> in trying to prolong them.
> I shall use my time."

November 30, 2003

"The Weight of Christmas Gifts"

All my life I have used Thanksgiving as the time to write holiday cards and to wrap gifts. No time for long walks, good movies, meaningful conversation. Maxie puts up with it and hauls the gifts to the post office.

However, I do need to rethink the number of gifts, their size and their weight. As Maxie points out every year, the postage sometimes exceeds the value of the gifts.

Gulp!

December 1, 2003

"WHITE RABBIT" You got me.

****

"Before I Die"
Before I die I want to accomplish three things:

1. Sail the Great Lakes on an ore boat.
2. Play the piano and sing a set in a run-down bar at midnight.
3. Drive an eighteen-wheeler across the country stopping at all the rest stops "For Truckers Only."

How can I make these happen?

"The Night Before"

Did you know that you prolong the life of your clothes if you do not wash or dry-clean them too often? Also, after each wearing, make sure you fold them carefully, hang them or press them. Many of my favorite outfits have years on them.

When I was in junior high, I would put out my clothes for the next day. Full skirts required ironing and the petticoats underneath were starched until they stood up by themselves. To this day I hang my clothes out for the next day, thus insuring they are ready to be matched with shoes, glasses, jewelry and scarves.

I love it when you visit me and we go through my closet and you are brutal with me. "Out," you shout as I try to convince you that some item still has life in it. And then you rearrange tops and bottoms in outlandish ways that work. I tend to wear the same combinations and you mix them up. I want you to know I follow your advice. So thanks. And thanks for asking me to do the same at your house when you try on your beautiful vintage wardrobe and we make tough decisions about their future and pile them in categories: "keep," "tailor," "consignment," "women's shelter."

It used to be said that the "clothes make the man." I wish more men would follow that rule. I do know that clothes make a huge difference for a woman. And I am not talking about spending a lot of money. Long ago Aunt Fay took me to Woolworth's Five and Dime Store. She said that selecting the right colored scarf at the dime store would bring compliments. She also taught Cousin Amy and me to walk tall.

You have wonderful taste, Monette, and look terrific in your glamorous wardrobe. And I love it that you spend more on the perfect jeans than you do on a dress for opening night, and you buy vintage clothing. You teach me a lot.

December 3, 2003

"What Do I Love About You?"

I love your passion for the theatre. "It's the thing that makes me happy."

I love it when you see an animal and exclaim with joy.

I love your beautiful, slender hands.

I love your unique, classy style.

I love your exploration of the spiritual.

I love how you problem solve. "What's the **real** problem here?"

I love your strong loyalties.

I love your political absolutes. "He's a moron!"

I love your intellect. "Why is that so?"

I love your originality. "Light your tiny study with a huge Italian chandelier."

I love your strength, courage, and the fact that you think for yourself.

I love remembering that you cried at the demise of a beautiful butterfly.

I love your honesty.

I love you.

December 4, 2003

"Sex...Under-rated!"

Max asked me if I had written any advice to you about sex yet. YIKES!!! Hadn't even thought about doing so, but here goes.

When I was in college and taking a course on health, Nana called from upstairs, "Make sure you read the chapter on sex." That was the extent of my home teaching. It was simply never discussed. Fortunately, my friend Janet had learned about the "deed" from her mother, when we were in sixth grade. Janet and I met at the corner to discuss it and were shocked at the thought of penetration.

From that revelation on, I was a late bloomer. Too Lutheran and too scared to "go all the way" until marriage. However, once I figured out satisfaction, I was convinced that sex was very under-rated.

Sex, it turns out, can ruin your life or help fulfill it. What other so personal an act can bring down a kingdom, start a war or break up a marriage? The very power of sex makes it under-rated.

And then there is the joy of sex, again under-rated. When you join your body with another, it is an extremely profound act and cannot ever be considered "casual."

I wasn't much better about sex education with you. When you were a senior in high school and planning a camping trip with your boyfriend, I remember picking up brochures from Planned Parenthood and giving them to you to read before the outing. You rolled your eyes and said, "Mother!" (translation: "You've got to be kidding." or "You're too late and too lame.")

So when it comes to sex, I hope for you the utter joy it can bring inside a loving, committed relationship. It simply doesn't work otherwise. And I hope you do a better job of "sex education" with your offspring if you ever decide to create new life.

"For the In-Between"

I know I wrote about death...must now write about dying. With so many relatives suffering with Alzheimer's, it is possible I will also. Here are a couple of thoughts. **Do not speak for me** if I can still speak. **Do not speak about me** if I can still hear. **But do speak to me** even if I cannot speak or apparently hear. The LAST thing to go is hearing and comprehension.

Keep me near a window, in the sunshine, and if possible near water. Hate sharing space with anyone but at the end, we all must. I like classical music (Sibelius, Ravel, Bach, Tchaikovsky, Debussy, Copeland, Chopin, Beethoven) but no Wagner. Of course include Max Morath's last CD. Also, Louis Armstrong, Edith Piaff, Ella Fitzgerald, the Carpenters, Mamma Mia. The Everly Brothers will bring a tear. Otherwise I prefer quiet.

My knees are shot from completing Grandma's Marathon when I was 45 with cousin Janice, so I prefer to have my legs outstretched when I sit. Books-on-CD are my favorite things. I LOVE A GOOD STORY! If there is money, I'd like my nails and hair done weekly. I like lipstick, and cream all over after a weekly bath; I hate showers but will comply if forced. I prefer being out-of-doors. A ride in a convertible with the top down will bring back high school memories and a chocolate malt will bring a smile. I love to take communion. I sleep best with a satin or silk pillowcase. I hate being around people who argue, talk all the time, or watch a lot of television. I love the fragrance of lily of the valley, lilac, and dill. I like my back to the wall. If I could pet a cat, I would be happy forever. Kindness works best for me.

Most likely I will end up in an institution with the television set on all day, in a ward with six women as nutty as me, and taking pills every four hours to keep me quiet. I will understand.

Reminder, I have a card in my wallet that states: "If there is no reasonable expectation of my recovery from extreme physical or mental disability - I direct that I be allowed to die and not be kept alive by artificial means and heroic measures"... etc. But no matter when I die, I will have lived life fully with just a few regrets.

December 6, 2003

"Romancing the Malt"
 Did you ever actually read our book, *Max Morath: The Road to Ragtime?* In it is Max's description of the perfect malt. Here it is:

THE TEN PRINCIPLES OF MALT

The Ice Cream
The Malt must be concocted of real ice cream, with a butter fat content of at least 18 per cent.

The Utensils
The ice cream must never be scooped with the fragile spherical blopper used for sundaes and cones, but with the Shovel scoop, the one that looks like it was hand-hammered from cast iron in 1906. The ice cream must be loaded into a large metal can, the Tin, never into a container of Styrofoam or paper.

The Milk
Whole milk is then added. Never ask for skim. Malting predates the recent wave of aversion to pleasure known as dieting.

The Consistency
One *drinks* a Malt. It should never be consumed through a straw. The straw is for soda pop and small children, who should be weaned away from it at an early age.

The Chocolate
The ideal Chocolate Malt (is there really any other flavor?) begins, of course, with vanilla ice cream. Plentiful chocolate syrup is then added for flavor, ideally squirted from a permanent fountain container. A seasoned Maltist listens for the squirting sound, the first of several aural rewards of Malting.
 continued...

DIANE FAY SKOMARS

December 7, 2003

"Romancing the Malt" continued...

The Malt Powder
A shocking fault of recent Malt is the increasing use of liquified malt extract, an abomination. The Perfect Malt is made with powdered Malt, plain and unflavored. And don't be bamboozled by the chocolate-flavored malt powders at the supermarket, dreadful concoctions suitable only in preparing bedtime drinks for infants and insomniacs. The grandeur of Malt - the mystery, actually - is in the intersections of raw Malt flavor, resembling no other, and the familiar sweetness and texture of the ice cream mix.

The Mixer
If you observe that a common kitchen blender is to be used to prepare your Malt, cancel at once. The True Malt is brought to its bubbling best only on a Hamilton-Beach unit. Its slender vertical stems, terminating in a mysterious disc the size of a quarter, some-how smooth and at the same time aerate the Malt. Look for the unique green and chrome exterior of the Hamilton-Beach, the mark of a busy and caring Malt Shoppe.

The Service
The finest malt, no matter how promising, is a failure if brought to the consumer in the glass only. The Tin, containing additional Malt, must also be brought to the Maltist. Its outer surface should already be sweating from the interface of the cold Malt within and humidity of the ambient air. Even in arid Colorado this condensation was impressive, and remains a Malt must. Try this test, proven by generations of Malting teenagers: your Malt's condensation should easily support a thumbed inscription of the initials of you and your steady around the outside of the Tin.

The Glass

The Malt must be presented in a real glass, heavy, flaring from its graceful, beveled base to the smooth circle at its top, where your eager lips will meet your Malt. I once watched a young woman in (name withheld), Oklahoma, prepare for me what promised to be a Ten, the Perfect Malt. She had it all:

"Romancing the Malt" continued
rich, thick vanilla ice cream, bountiful chocolate syrup. (I could hear it squirt into the Tin) a healthy double dollop of classic powdered Malt; just the right amount of whole milk, poured from a quart bottle! With a practiced hand she mounted the mixture on a time-worn but immaculate Hamilton-Beach. I turned away, embarrassed by the tenderness I felt developing between us and my Malt. Moments later I turned back and watched in horror as she poured this treasure into a 12-ounce Styrofoam cup and emptied the Tin's remainder into the sink. I wept.

Hearing the Malt
Newcomers to Malt may be unaware of this phenomenon. Raised on the insipid stepchild of Malt known as the "shake," they have never *heard* a Malt. They are accustomed to the boring, soundless flow of the soft ice cream shake into a waxed paper cup, a fast-food ersatz consumed by rote and without passion. The Perfect Malt sings "blah-LUMP, bah-LUMP" to you, as the still-lumpy mixture first descends into the glass. Here the art of the Malt Maker meets its ultimate test. The Tin must be removed from the Hamilton-Beach at just the right moment. Liquefaction has taken place, but a few strategic blobs of ice cream must remain to produce the perfect "bah-LUMP."

****

Max goes on to write about the future of the Malt and describes membership in the National Order of the Malt! I love this essay. It is quintessential Max Morath. By the way, in all our years of marriage, I have been with Max only twice when he found a "9" on a 10 point scale for a perfect malt. Once was up the North Shore

of Lake Superior at the Rustic Inn at Castle Danger and the other
was at Annie's Parlor in Dinkytown, Minneapolis.

DIANE FAY SKOMARS

"A Hungry Belly Has No Ears" (world-wide saying)

Have you ever been truly hungry with no prospects of food? It happened to me only once when I was in my twenties. I had food for the pets but my cupboards were bare, and I wouldn't get paid for a couple of days and I had no money. My parents were out of the country and my husband was in the military and I was too proud to ask a friend or neighbor.

So I prayed.

The next day, relatives arrived and realized my situation and went to the grocery store and made meals without ceremony or incrimination. I never, ever forgot how I felt through this incident (embarrassed, humbled, scared, stupid, hungry, and very grateful to these relatives). And I never allowed it to happen again in my life.

THINK of how it feels for children and adults EVERY DAY when there is no food and no prospects for food or a job. It breaks my heart.

Food is never so important than when you have none. And, indeed, a hungry belly doesn't want speeches, it wants food. Thank God for food banks.

Monette, I ask you again. Have you ever been truly hungry with no prospects of food? If so, what did you do, what did you learn?

December 10, 2003

"This I Believe"

I believe God is good.

I do not believe in capital punishment.

I do believe in justice.

Women know best about reproduction and I trust them.

The media is responsible for perpetuating most negative things in this world.

Nature holds essential truths.

The process is as important as the end result.

Love between two people is the point.

The Internet will ultimately do more harm than good.

Hard work belongs to everyone in equal measure, as they are able.

In the end our differences will not be about race, but class. The losers will be those who do not learn to share.

Rights are rights. Responsibilities are another important matter.

It is never about power or might, speed or size, volume or supremacy.

We are brothers and sisters of all living things.

Although I am passionate about my country, I am a citizen of the world, too.

Figure out what you believe, why you believe it, and then act on it.

"Tell Me More"

Our friend Claudia told me that she often asks friends to tell her more, after they have shared a story. This invitation can open new doors to understanding and can get underneath a story.

Try it when you are listening to someone. "Tell me more."

December 12, 2003

"I Know What I Am Supposed to Do But It Is Difficult"

It is clear that I am supposed to just listen when you are having a rough time and not comment, not tell you what to do, and above all not to pass judgment. Because this is YOUR LIFE!

But once in a while I want to shout, "Look around at all your blessings! Be glad therein. Love yourself! When you are blue, take a walk; invite a stranger to coffee; join a church or meditation group; enroll in classes; work at the Women's Shelter or Food Bank or Humane Society; or get on your knees and pray."

But I am too cool a mom to do so. I am supposed to just listen.

December 13, 2003

"Bobbles, Bangles, and Bracelets"

I wear nine bracelets every day. The only downside to wearing them occurs when I go through security at the airport. Otherwise, they are my friends. They remind me of:

1. A gold bangle gift from a trip to Alice Springs, Australia
2. Our tenth anniversary with "Maxi Taxi" and "Diane Fay" engraved
3. "The Lord is my Shepherd" bangle from a friend
4. A month in Norway commemorative
5. A "Sister" bracelet from Pat and Buzz
6. A Viking-inspired design in silver, from my wonderful Finnish relatives
7. Purchased my leopard bracelet in San Gimignano, Italy
8. John Hardy's gold and silver gift from you (Bali)
9. A second gold bangle; I bought this one in Israel

The upside to wearing nine bracelets? When I want to lose five pounds, I remove them.

December 14, 2003

"Thank You"

It will be so good to be with you at Christmas. Thank you for the invitation. Max is sorry not to join me but you seem to understand he simply wants to stay home.

You'll draw the name of our Christmas family at the Salvation Army and we'll shop at Target finding just the right items for each family member. We'll race home and wrap the gifts and bring them to the center.

Can't wait to make our Christmas Eve dinner including prime rib with Sheldon's special gravy, elegant potatoes, haricot vert, Dot's cupcakes. We will attend the festive All Saints Episcopal Church service and sing our hearts out.

And then there's the 26th. Up at 6 a.m. and at Target by 7 a.m. to pick up discounted holiday items. Then we make the rounds to about eight stores in Old Town, purchasing cards and gifts for next year. We'll have a great lunch and get our nails done.

I love Christmas with you!

"Recycle"

When I learned that birds were dying because they were trying to digest our discarded plastic, I got serious about recycling. The way I see it, we can recycle just about everything in our life but our loved ones. Examples:

1. When you receive a bouquet of flowers, keep them and admire them for 24 hours feeding them ice cubes, and pass them on to someone not likely to get a bouquet.
2. Each season, sort out your clothes and send one third on their way to friends, relatives or a women's shelter.
3. Check your cupboards for extra cans, pasta, and jars to bring to the food bank each month before they expire.
4. Begin giving each book you read to someone else explaining it is lightly used.
5. When someone admires a piece of jewelry or a scarf you are wearing and you can live without it, give it to that person on the spot.
6. Recycle wine you have been given but cannot use. (I believe one bottle of wine went between five households before it came back to us!)
7. Separate paper/cans/bottles/plastics for recycling.
8. Use no bottled water. Use filtered water. Use reusable grocery bags.
9. Buy glass food containers and not plastic bags.
10. If you hate sponsoring a garage sale, give your stuff to a neighborhood garage sale and walk away from the items and the cash. Be grateful you got rid of your possessions and remind the sellers you don't want anything back or anything for it.

"Asking for Help"

After a recent health scare, I learned that it is hard for me to ask for help. I heard your lecture. "It's not that you **can't** ask for help, Mother, but rather you **don't** ask for help." I get it but I hate it.

The incident that led to this lesson was: although I woke up with severe stomach pains, I sent Max with his coffee guys and drove myself to the doctor. Was put in the E.R. and was given morphine. After a series of tests and being told not to drive, I drove myself home. Patients next to me had family and friends with them. I was peaceful and happy to be alone. And the staff was marvelous.

I didn't want to bother you or Maxie or Lucy with my troubles, but I hear you. I will try to learn to ask for help. P.S. Reports came back negative. I thank God.

Lesson: listen to your body and when there is unmanageable pain, tell others and seek help.

"Windy, Buzzy and Dolly Photographed by Pops" (We all had nick-names.)

December 18, 2003

"What on Earth Did the Lindbergh Kidnapping Have to Do with Me?"

I could never understand why my childhood bedroom window was nailed shut. My parents told me that after the Lindbergh baby was kidnapped, parents nailed windows shut in their child's room. The answer made me feel safe but strange. Why would anyone come to Duluth, Minnesota to kidnap an unknown child?

To this day I open every window I can.

DIANE FAY SKOMARS

"Looking Back and Having No Enemies"

A while ago I heard an interview of two famous musicians, one female and one male. The female asserted that the goal in life is to look back and have no enemies. The male disagreed and said that the goal in life is to look back and know your enemies.

I agree with the woman who felt it is best to have no enemies.

What do you believe?

"Cranberry Cake"

    2 tablespoons melted butter
1 cup sugar
2 cups flour
2 teaspoons baking powder
1 cup milk
2 cups whole, raw cranberries
Sauce:
1/2 cup butter
1 cup sugar
3/4 cup whipping cream (room temperature)

Mix cake ingredients together. Pour into 8x8 inch pan and bake at 350 degrees for 40 minutes.

Sauce:
Melt butter and remove from stove. Add sugar and return to stove until sugar dissolves. Add cream and cook sauce 10 minutes. Serve hot over pieces of cake.

You grew up on this one. Always brings raves. From friend, JoAnn. (JoAnn and Bob pass on the best books to us; they are one special couple.)

December 21, 2003

"To Die Peacefully"
"We cannot hope to die peacefully if our lives have been full of violence, or if our minds have mostly been agitated by emotions like anger, attachment, or fear. So if we wish to die well, we must learn how to live well. Hoping for a peaceful death, we must cultivate peace in our mind, and in our way of life." The Dalai Lama

Monette, you have within you a kind of a barometer that lets you know if your life is in order. Listen to every signal your body and soul transmits. A headache is one such signal but so is laughter and so is peaceful sleep.

Often bad food does not create a stomachache but rather bad judgment can create the ache. And clarity of thinking when motivated by love, gives you a sense of wellbeing. It is more than knowing right from wrong, but understanding the nuances that make it so.

Death is already in preparation. Just look at your life.

"Twelve Days of Christmas"

Remember how we sing the "Twelve Days of Christmas" every year in the car? We can never remember the words correctly so here they are:

On the first day of Christmas
my true love sent to me:
A Partridge in a Pear Tree
On the second day of Christmas...**2 Turtle Doves**...
On the third day of Christmas...**3 French Hens**...
On the fourth day of Christmas...**4 Calling Birds**...
On the fifth day of Christmas...**5 Golden Rings**...
On the sixth day of Christmas...**6 Geese a-Laying**...
On the seventh day of Christmas...**7 Swans a-Swimming**...
On the eighth day of Christmas...**8 Maids a-Milking**...
On the ninth day of Christmas...**9 Ladies Dancing**...
On the tenth day of Christmas...**10 Lords a-Leaping**...
On the eleventh day of Christmas...**11 Pipers Piping**...
On the twelfth day of Christmas...**12 Drummers Drumming**...

Let's get it right this year!

"To Remember Me"

In her lovely book, *Live it to the Brim*, my friend Libby Gill quotes from Robert Test's reading "I Will Live Forever."

"The day will come when my body will lay upon a white sheet neatly tucked under four corners of a mattress located in a hospital busily occupied with the living and the dying. At a certain moment a doctor will determine that my brain has ceased to function and that, for all intents and purposes, my life has stopped.

When that happens, do not attempt to instill artificial life into my body by the use of a machine. And don't call this my deathbed. Let it be called the Bed of Life, and let my body be taken from it to help others lead fuller lives. Give my sight to the man who has never seen a sunrise, a baby's face or love in the eyes of a woman.

Give my heart to a person whose own heart has caused nothing but endless days of pain.

Give my blood to the teenager who was pulled from the wreckage of his car so that he might live to see his grandchildren play.

Give my kidneys to one who depends on a machine to exist from week to week.

Take my bones, every muscle, every fiber and nerve in my body and find a way to make a crippled child walk. Explore every corner of my brain. Take my cells, if necessary, and let them grow so that someday, a speechless boy will shout at the crack of a bat and a deaf girl will hear the sound of rain against her window.

Burn what is left of me and scatter the ashes in the wind to help the flowers grow. If you must bury something let it be my faults, my weaknesses, and
all my prejudices against my fellow man. And finally, give my sins to the devil and my soul to God."

December 24, 2003

"Have I Taught You Everything I Know?"

Half way through the journal I had to answer, "Of course I have!" But I kept writing anyhow because it started to feel like a conversation. And you, my dear, have taught me plenty, and I thank you for that.

I get tearful remembering September 11, 2001 and weep for those who died by flames, flight or fright, and those who survived barely, and those who responded at risk to their own lives. It was the worst of times, and through our heroes, the best of times.

Now, up from ashes, we pause to look back and to realize our country still functions in spite of our lumps and bumps. Our core values seem to prevail although they are tested from time to time, and our commitment to freedom from tyranny and injustice seems strong.

I also look back on the day my world shrank from feeling like I owned New York as I walked to my work place on that beautiful morning, to a tiny studio where I felt trapped, alone and frightened to death. Thank you for being there for me.

Our story is our own, then and forever more.

December 25, 2003

"It is Finished"

I cannot put it off any longer. I must wrap up this journal and tuck it under the tree, way in back.

You don't have to read it.

You don't have to comment on it.

But **you** might want to write one for me some day with the same title: *Have I Taught You Everything I Know?*

"Ten Years Later"

At this writing, I have been retired for over three years and, as promised, I have readied this book for publication. When I visited you a year ago, I told you the following: "I have an idea for this book. I will create one perfect copy with original art and colored photographs on beautiful paper. You and I will each come up with a list of 25 women friends and we will send the book around to those 50 friends advising each to keep it five days and then mail to the next person on the list. That way, when you get it back, the book will have been held and blessed by 50 fabulous women."

"That's the dumbest idea I have ever heard of, Mother! The first woman will misplace it and keep it three weeks, and the second one will drop it in the water on vacation in Jamaica!"

And so we have self published this book ten years after its writing. A lot has happened since I spent the year of 2003 penning a lesson a day for you. There has been your wedding, Finnfest 2008 with Jeanne, road trips with Lucy, health scares, adventure travels with Cynthia, semi-weekly bridge games with Ken and Jackie, retirement, University for Seniors, consulting in England, the addition of more bracelets, delivering Meals on Wheels, loss, change, sorrow, and plenty of joy. I thank God that you and I are still close, communicating almost daily even if it now includes text messaging and Face Time.

It has been a good journey to revisit the pages of a mother's advice and wishes for her daughter. I will always be grateful to you, Max, and Christine for help editing *Have I Taught You Everything I Know?* and to Lucy for technical assistance. And I want to thank Cat Esme who purred encouragement all those early morning hours while I typed away getting the entries into the computer. Only she knows the private agony and the ecstasy of my project.

And so I leave you with this one last thought: "If you give it away, it comes back a hundred fold."

Diane Fay Skomars,
Mother-at Large

CPSIA information can be obtained at www.ICGtesting.com
Printed in the USA
BVOW02s0610141015

422339BV00001B/1/P